What Should I Believe?

Sorting Out Today's Bewildering Christian Beliefs

Hubert F. Beck

Publishing House
St. Louis

Concordia Publishing House, St. Louis, Missouri

Copyright © 1980 Concordia Publishing House
All rights reserved.
ISBN: 0-570-03800-6
Manufactured in the United States of America.

Table of Contents

Introduction

It was little more than a passing remark at one of our Sunday evening fellowship suppers. It wasn't even directed to me at the time, in fact. I did happen to hear Sue say something to one of the other students about so many new religions these days. Sue was a senior who had been to chapel on occasion but who frankly admitted that for the most part coming to church didn't "turn her on." I heard her remark but didn't think much about it, and the conversation was not pursued further at that time.

Several days later, however, Sue came to me seeming rather troubled. She asked me directly at that time about why so many new religions were starting up.

I wasn't sure what she meant by "new religions," for I hear people talking about denominations as different "religions," about cults as "new religions," and sometimes one can hear different manifestations of faith spoken of as "kinds of religions." So I asked her to explain herself more thoroughly.

"Well, let me tell you about some people who have talked with me in just the last week or so.

"First of all there was this girl who was trying to tell me that all the signs of the end of the world were being fulfilled. She told me that if I would read the Bible and watch the newspaper headlines that I would see all of the Biblical prophecies coming true right before my eyes.

"A couple days later a fellow was telling me about how he had been born with one leg shorter than the other by two inches, but that his short leg had been lengthened in a special prayer meeting a week earlier. He even invited me to come with him to another meeting tomorrow evening, and I don't know whether to go or not. He says they speak in tongues and experience all kinds of healings and gifts of special power from the Holy Spirit.

"Well, I thought I had heard about enough for one week when still someone else started telling me about the thousand years of

4

glory that would soon come when Jesus would return for the—I can't even remember what she called it!"

"Millennium," I offered.

"Yes!" she said with some surprise. "Do you know what I'm talking about? I surely don't! I was never taught any of that in confirmation class!"

"There are a few other things that you could have named, in fact, if that is what you are talking about when you speak of 'new religions,' " I replied. "I wasn't sure what you meant, but you're not really speaking of new religions. You're talking about different forms of religious expression within the framework of the Christian faith. They've all been around in one form or another for a long time . . . some of them since the time of Christ and before, in fact! But they show up and disappear at different times and in different ways, only to reappear and show themselves in new forms again at later times."

"You said there were still other things I could've mentioned?" Her expression indicated that she didn't know if she could stand to hear still other people surprise her with things like this. But it also invited at least a suggestion of some other expressions of religious faith that could cross her path.

So I ventured to mention at least a couple more to her so that she wouldn't be caught completely off-guard in the future. "Have you ever been asked if you were 'saved'?"

"Of course," she answered. "that's a common question for Christians to ask people. There's nothing new about that!"

"You might be surprised to find how 'new' it is to ask that question . . . at least in the way it's usually phrased and discussed today. Nearly always the question that goes with it is something like, 'When did you become a Christian?' It's almost as though they were testing the authenticity of your answer."

Now Sue looked a bit troubled. "Yes, you're right about that. I *have* sometimes wondered about that, for I really can't say much about that except to refer to my baptism."

"Why do you need to refer to anything else?" I asked.

"Well . . . they seem to want me to say something else. And those who ask me can usually refer to some particular time, so I sort of feel that I ought to also."

"There you see the problem of that kind of expression. Although the Christian faith has always understood faith to be personal, it has never really found it wise to 'test' any affirmation of faith with such questions as 'When were you saved?' or 'Have you made your decision for Christ?' If you let questions like that bother you, it isn't

5

too hard to bring on a crisis of faith for yourself. I've counseled more than one person who was caught in such a critical reexamination of his or her faith."

Sue nodded her head and said that she could see how this would be true, for she herself had on occasion wondered if she really was a Christian since she couldn't seem to speak of any experiences like some of her friends spoke about.

"Have you ever been confronted by people who make you wonder if you really believe the Bible?" I asked, going a step further.

"I'm not sure what you mean," Sue responded. "I know that I don't know my Bible as well as I should. Is that what you mean?"

"Not really. Let me put it another way. You've already run into them in one way when you heard the person talking about the millennium. That's a very literal reading of several passages in the 20th chapter of the Book of Revelation. You ran into it again when you were told to read the newspapers alongside certain selected quotes from the prophets. There are still other ways it can show up, though.

"Have you ever been asked why you worshiped on Sunday instead of Saturday, the day of worship set aside in the Old Testament? Or have you ever been challenged on the kind of diet you eat? Some want to point to certain Biblical restraints against things like pork or certain other kinds of things to eat."

Sue had never really run into questions of this sort. So I related the question back again to those who want to ask if she believes this or that thing quite literally. Frequently such questions will center on events of the last time or what heaven or hell is like or some detail of the narrative in Scripture. "You begin to feel that you're saved more by believing certain passages in the Bible than by believing in Christ as your Savior. When you keep listening to people like that, you somehow begin to think that you're godly because you know how to quote Bible passages rather than because you've been caught up into the sweep of God's grace. I call this the 'back to the Bible' syndrome."

"But we *should* base all our teachings on the Bible," Sue objected.

"Ah, yes! That we should! But the Bible must always be used in the right way. If the Bible is made to be just a rule book or a book of coded messages which people are to decode and believe so they will 'know' things other people don't know, it has been badly abused. That's very different from using the Bible as the only source of our teaching and life."

6

"I think I see what you mean," she conceded. "But I'm not sure that I've ever quite thought of it that way."

"Since we've been taught to honor the Bible and to base all our teachings on it, we frequently don't question anybody too much who claims to use it. But we need to watch carefully so the Bible isn't twisted and turned to serve any old purpose a person chooses to use it for. It has a life of its own, to be sure, but its life is God-breathed and must 'swim in the channel of history' if it is to serve the purpose for which God gave it to us. It's an age-old problem."

The discussion went on like this for a while. It returned to the question of why so many "new religions" (as Sue continued to call them) or "different religious expressions" (as I preferred to call them) were emerging on today's religious scene. I noted that not many, if any, were really new. They were old teachings (many of them declared heresy long ago) dressed up in modern clothing. Sue wanted to pursue the discussion, and we did to some extent in weeks to come.

But the end of that conversation was the beginning of this book! As I mulled over her questions and remembered how many, many times they had been asked of me by so many people in so many situations, I wondered if perhaps a little "treatise" on each of the things we had brought up in our conversation might not be helpful to many people. Perhaps our subsequent discussions played into the making of this book, but that first conversation became the basic outline.

Many other questions, discussions, and reflections got caught up into the substance of what is in this book, of course, for these bewildering beliefs current today take on many forms. A large number of them have their origin in very old notions that have repeatedly been propagated—and rejected—throughout the centuries since the time of Christ. It is our hope that these pages can help readers to understand why these forms of religious expression so fascinate people that they will not die . . . and at the same time will help all of us to understand why they are in their own way such treacherously dangerous ideas to play with.

1

Religion by
Anticipation and Fulfillment

The future is always an interesting subject.

At every turn of the year one can pick up almost any newspaper or magazine and find portions of it devoted to predictions of what the new year holds in store for us. Psychics write column after column about what they "see" for the next year; economic prophets tell us whether inflation will continue or a depression is about to set in and what all that means for investors; politicians forecast the major legislation that will occupy the attention of the nation—on and on the projections go for the year ahead.

So much ink is devoted to such articles because the readers of these periodicals "eat it up." After all, the future is where we are going to live, so we like to have an idea of what it's going to be like to move into the territory of the future.

In a way we are more obsessed with the future than previous generations of mankind have been. It's not that people were disinterested in the future in past generations. Change didn't occur so rapidly in the past, however, and the future was usually seen as a continuation of the present. Major changes were not so generally expected, and so the future seemed a bit more secure and less threatening than it does for us today.

The changes we anticipate in these days of the late 20th century are far more extensive than whether the rain and sun will appear at proper times for the crops. They are changes under the direct control of human beings, and they are happening at such increasingly rapid rates that we sometimes feel the whole world is spinning dizzily out of control. We hardly need to detail these many major changes for any modern-day reader. Nor need we detail the way these changes have created a certain fear of the future (even while at the same time they hold an almost magic fascination for us as we see them unfolding before us!) that ranges as widely as nuclear war

9

to spiraling inflation with fears of subsequent depression to some medical accident that will either flood the world with some aberrant gene that could destroy humankind or could create a monster that would frighten us to death. We in Western society find ourselves involved with a culture that requires continually accelerating technology for survival on the one hand and that sees the same technology as a fearful enemy on the other hand.

No wonder we live our lives with our eyes on the future today rather than on the past as was typical of most previous generations!

No wonder, also, that religion has suddenly turned its eyes to the future with a new emphasis on anticipating what God has in store for His creation!

The Bible is full of "forward looking" passages that can become the building blocks for all kinds of "predicters" telling us almost anything they want to! How does one sort through the myriad of "future peddlers" that have flooded the religious market of today? Knowing full well that the prophetic figures were people who preached their strong messages to Israel on the strength of future anticipations as well as on what God had done in the past, we cannot simply ignore the future orientation of the Scriptures. But one cannot simply accept anything and everything that a person wants to say about the future so long as he has a Bible passage in hand that at least in some remote sense of the term seems to coincide with "signs" that appear in today's headlines.

You can probably relate to the dilemma of a parishioner who came into his pastor's office looking for guidance after he had been talking with someone who told him that the very existence of Israel again in today's world was the sign that the end of the world was very near.

"Pastor, the way this fellow talked the Bible is a regular roadmap for the end of the world. According to him everything that's happened in the last 50 years was predicted in the Bible, and he has it figured out from here until Jesus' coming again what all will take place. What's this all about? I haven't heard anything about things like that in church."

As his pastor told it to me, that was the introduction to some very serious discussion about the nature of prophecy.

Precisely because the future seems so unsettled in so many ways, more and more people are seeking knowledge about what the future holds in store. Of course, nobody *knows* what lies in the future, so one must either do a lot of guesswork or else one must have a definite "roadmap" of the future. It's not hard to make the Bible such a "roadmap" rather than a sourcebook of faith, and so one hears more and more from people who take the words of the Bible and make of them a way to determine the future before it happens. If *God's* knowledge is at our disposal, then we can plan precisely for what is to come!

The question, though, is whether this is even remotely the original intention of Scripture—to give us detailed knowledge of what is yet to take place.

Many people think it is that because of the many prophecies in the Bible.

"The prophets foretold the destruction of Jerusalem, the captivity of Israel, the return of Judah, the coming of the Messiah—why could they not have foretold what is to happen in the late 20th century?" The question was a very serious one, as was evident by the intensity of the man's tone of voice. He was trying to get me to read one of the tracts he was handing out at the airport.

"I don't argue with whether God could foretell something about our day and age," I replied. "But that's not what the Bible is all about. The prophets were 'preachers' to their day. They were 'proclaiming' the Word of the Lord to those who were their contemporaries. They were not standing in a vacuum predicting things that would happen centuries later for the most part. And even when they spoke of things to come in distant times it had to do with the age of the Messiah, the coming of the Savior. These were messianic hopes that they expressed, having been assured by God's guiding Spirit that their hopes were not in vain and that God Himself would put flesh and blood on those hopes."

"It's as plain as day if you'll just let the Bible talk to you," he insisted. "Ever since Communism came into power as the great 'Antichrist,' the signs of the end of the world have become more and more evident. If you'll just take this and read it, it will prove to you that we'll soon see the second coming of Christ."

Once you started talking with him it was hard to get away from him. But it was equally evident that there was no "discussion" possible. He had his mind made up, and he was out to convince anybody who would listen to him.

That is a common thing today, whether in transportation centers where people are handing out literature or whether at the corner grocery store where someone is attempting to convince you of the imminence of the end. Always the discussion focuses on "the signs of the times," and nearly always the central sign revolves around the restoration of the land of Israel to the Jewish people.

11

That is no accident from the Biblical point of view, for at least two reasons. First of all, a great deal of prophecy did indeed center on Israel's return from captivity and the restoration of the land, which gives much material to work with for anyone looking for predictive passages out of the prophets. Second, the possession of the land of Israel was a crucial concern throughout the entire Old Testament and was therefore a topic of great interest under any circumstances to the people of Israel.

Since so much attention is indeed devoted to the land of Israel, therefore, it would seem a natural focus for those who look for "signs" in the first few decades after Israel was again restored following many, many centuries of nonexistence. Put that event into the swirl of a rapidly changing world where people want certainty about the future in the face of great threats and even potential disasters, and it easily becomes the center of the "signs" that make the future predictable. If God could predict many centuries earlier that Israel would be restored, it is argued, could He not also have predicted other things about our age? We shall continue these considerations under another heading in the next chapter, but for now let's stop a bit and try to examine this reasoning a little more closely.

It has probably become evident by now that the question we are dealing with revolves around two poles.

The first pole has to do with the nature of the Biblical literature as such. What is the original intention of the Biblical writers? Were they interested in "foreseeing" as much world history as possible? Were they "future oriented" out of curiosity about what was yet to come? Were they perhaps primarily *satisfiers* of curiosity for generations of people yet to be born? Or was their intention something quite other than the satisfaction of curiosity? If they had other intentions, what were they? These and similar questions will be dealt with at some length in ch. 5, but they are introduced here since they have become so obvious.

It is the second pole around which the questions of this chapter revolve that will occupy us for the present, though. And that has to do with the nature of prophecy and the prophetic office. What was the task and intention of the prophets introduced to us in Scripture?

Angie, newly married and working her husband through school, had been attending a Bible study group on Tuesday evenings at the home of a friend who lived in the next apartment complex. Somehow the group had gotten off into a discussion of prophecies at about the same time a major world crisis was ticking off in the Middle East, so the conversation was particularly disturbing to her. When she came to me it was apparent that she was in considerable distress, for she had become convinced that the Bible had predicted what was happening and she saw it as the foreboding event that would be followed shortly by worldwide catastrophe.

I could hardly deny that worldwide catastrophe was a possibility, for in today's world almost any major crisis in any part of the world can threaten to trigger a universal holocaust. Without being unduly pessimistic, one must constantly recognize that possibility as reality.

"It's quite another thing, though," I said to Angie, "to tie such threats to Biblical prophecies. To do so is to make the prophets basically predicters of future world events. Very many people confuse 'prophecy' with 'prediction' and thereby do grave injustices to great men of God such as Amos, Isaiah, Jeremiah, and the apostle John in the New Testament."

"But they *did* make predictions and the predictions came true," she objected. "We studied the whole history of that time and found that they did know what they were talking about."

That is an undeniable fact, as I confessed. "But the prophets in the Old Testament had a much, much larger task than merely the making of a few predictions here and there. Their basic task was to interpret the events of contemporary history for the people of their day. To be sure, they addressed themselves primarily to the rulers of Israel, since Israel had been so uniquely chosen by God to carry a specially appointed role among the nations of the world. But they did not ignore world history in the process of such major addresses to their own rulers and people.

"They were most intensely concerned about the way their own country responded to the needs of justice over against the needy, and they called for mercy over against the oppressed. By the grace of God, they looked across the span of time to see far-reaching implications in the local and momentary decisions made by those who held power in their own country.

"It was in the process of rebuking the people for their unconcern about the needy that many of their predictions were made. Their predictions were generally tied to the nature of the present actions of their countrymen, although there certainly were remarkable Messianic prophecies that looked to the coming New Testament age. But most of what the prophets said concerned the fact that God had made a covenant with this nation of Israel and had given this land to them with the understanding that they would be a 'light to the nations,' showing how a nation under God would live. It was to be, in short, a 'holy nation.' (The word 'holy' means 'separated out' and indicated how Israel was different and 'set apart' from all other nations.) If or when it ceased fulfilling that function, it forfeited its right to exist.

"These were the conditions under which the predictions were made, and in one sense of the term many of them can almost be understood as 'common sense predictions' that anybody with eyes to see could have made. They were based on the common knowledge available to anybody acquainted with the history of Israel.

"Yet this is not to take away from the nature of these prophetic utterances as 'inspired,' for the prophets quite apparently had a vision far exceeding that available to the common person. Somehow they were able—and this is where the divine guidance of God shows up—to see in the common, ordinary, everyday events of their time the stuff that was the making of Israel's undoing, and also to see the grace and love of God which would not finally abandon His people. What seems apparent by hindsight is not nearly so apparent when you stand in the middle of a situation. And they had to stand in the middle of the deteriorating conditions of Israel and speak a hard word that nobody in Israel wanted to hear or believe. They had to open their own eyes to what everybody wanted to deny. That, and the grace of God they also kept pointing to, took a vision granted by God Himself.

"Then you're saying that their predictions basically had to do with their own day and age?" It was plain that Angie was as distressed by that implication as she had been by the ones that first brought her to me.

"Some of them did have to do almost entirely with their own day and age, but it is plain that in many cases their words had taken on far more than merely local and contemporaneous meanings. Their vision stretched so far across the ages that they could see in some God-inspired way that whatever happened to Israel in their day would have something to do with the whole of world history in the future, especially with the coming of the Messiah and the New Testament age.

"They were remarkable men, these people of God who were led by His Spirit to see so widely and so far ahead at the same time they had to address the people of their own day.

"Putting all this together, I'm trying to say this: They were not speaking predictions into a vacuum. They saw that whatever happened to Israel had, through the Messiah, an effect in a very long-range way on the whole world, and that God was involved in the totality of this continuing history both of Israel and the world. So, while addressing their contemporaries and the situations within which they found themselves, they saw beyond all this in many ways and anticipated things yet to come. The New Testament gathers all this together as it makes plain that what seemed so unclear in terms of just what it was that God would be doing among and for people had now been made clear in Christ. I think one of the clearest statements of this is made by Peter when he says: 'The prophets who prophesied of the grace that was to be yours searched and inquired about this salvation; they inquired what person or time was indicated by the Spirit of Christ within them when predicting the sufferings of Christ and the subsequent glory. It was revealed to them that they were serving not themselves but you, in the things which have now been announced to you by those who preached the good news to you through the Holy Spirit sent from heaven, things into which angels long to look.' " (1 Peter 1:10-12)

"Then why do you say that none of the present events were predicted? If the prophets looked past their circumstances and saw into the future, how can you say that they didn't foresee our present-day events and predict them?"

"The intention of the prophets never seems to go beyond two things as you read the Scriptures:

"Their first intention seems plain—to warn Israel against its waywardness and to predict, if one wants to use that term, what the eventual outcome of such waywardness would be if pursued to its bitter end. That's their immediate intention.

"Their second intention seems to be to look beyond that to a time when God would intersect with human history in some unique way. That's envisioned as a time of renewal and restoration, marked by 'new heavens and a new earth,' to use a phrase frequently employed. That would be the time when all of Israel's history would come into focus and take on a unique meaning among all nations of the world. As Christians, we see that event in the birth, life, suffering, death, resurrection, and ascension of Christ, in whom the whole of Israel's history is relived and given its fullest meaning.

"Beyond those two intentions one cannot find any real thrust of prophetic direction or intent. They had their eyes keenly focused in these directions, and there is no hint that they were interested in the unfolding of world history simply for the sake of satisfying curiosity."

15

"But Pastor," Angie protested again, "it's not merely for the sake of satisfying curiosity that we were trying to see how the present-day events fulfill all the prophecies of the past. We're serious about searching for God's intentions for us today, and all these fulfillments are signs of the times in which we live, for surely these are the 'end times.' Every sign points to it."

"That we live in the end times is the testimony of the whole New Testament. It's been true ever since then that we live in the 'end times,' and virtually every generation since then has been sure that the end of the world was imminent—within days or months or at best years.

"But it's not for us to second-guess God's time, when even Jesus said: 'Of that day and hour no one knows, not even the angels of heaven, nor the Son, but the Father only' (Matt. 24:36). He distinctly warned us, in fact, before His ascension, against expending too much effort in determining such 'signs of the end' when He said: 'It is not for you to know times or seasons which the Father has fixed by His own authority' (Acts 1:7).

"For that reason I'm concerned about too much emphasis placed on 'verifying' or 'affirming' the Bible by looking for fulfilled prophecies. What happens, for example, if someone shows you a passage and interprets it in such a way that some event is to be expected in world history within a short time... within your lifetime ... and then it never happens. Does that mean that God failed ... or that God deceived you ... or that the Bible is untrustworthy ... or that other things we read in the Bible won't come true either?

"Now I'm aware," I went on hurriedly as I saw Angie start to respond, "that the response immediately is to say that none of that is true but that the interpreter had read the Bible wrongly rather than to say that the Bible itself was wrong. The more opportunity you give yourself, though, to question what you read in the Bible the more you place yourself squarely in the way of doubt and uncertainty and eventually of unbelief itself.

"That is not to say that it will inevitably happen, but none of us is so strong in faith that we can afford to put ourselves into a way that potentially will weaken or destroy our faith."

The conversation continued for quite some time, and perhaps already we have belabored that particular discussion here.

It is important, though, to recognize that "religion by anticipation and fulfillment" is a treacherous path. To build our faith on a series of supposedly predictive passages related to contemporary world events pulled together from various and sundry places in

Scripture without regard for their context and then reassembled piecemeal by someone who is trying to prove that God can foretell the future is to build our faith on shaky ground at best.

God can, indeed, foretell events. The question is not whether He can but whether foretelling the events of our time is the nature of the prophetic task of Scripture. The Scriptures are honored as God's Word because in them authoritative understandings about how God relates to and deals with people, especially in the Christ, are revealed. It is for such things we look, along with the related questions of how God's dealing with His "holy" people, "separated out" from all other peoples of the world, can guide us in our decision making and activities as the "holy" and "separated out" people of God today. The Scriptures, therefore, are honored by our reverent study of what God has promised and done for us in the Christ, gleaning from that climactic act of God what His will for us in our day might be.

To look for the fulfillments of signs, though, is to make Scripture a roadmap for the future in a way it was not intended to be. Whether there will really be 10 members of the Common Market as a revival of the old Roman Empire (as some writers try to tell us on the basis of interpretations of some of these supposedly "predictive passages") is of little consequence. Whether the Common Market has more or less or exactly 10 members will not be the difference between whether we can rely on the Scriptures as God's Word or not. The emergence of Israel as a nation again is an important event in world history, but that single event neither affirms nor denies the truth of Scripture nor does it have anything to say ultimately about whether God is to be trusted or not. He would still be trusted even if Israel had not reemerged as a nation.

As we noted at the beginning of this chapter, it should come as no surprise to us that there is a great interest in the future in the framework of our modern culture. It is a legitimate concern to question the direction of our society. In that sense we all carry a certain "prophetic" task of evaluating and guiding as much as is possible in a democratic society the future of our country and with it the future of the world.

Placing our faith in Scripture as a roadmap into that future, however, is a misguided effort. All around us the anxiety about the future is leading more and more people to search for such security as would anchor them in the midst of rapid change by looking for God's intentions coded in some obscure way in the words of Holy Scripture so that they can "know" what will happen and, so to speak, be at the

17

right place at the right time when these "predicted" events occur.

Our faith that God will be present in the future is not based on decoding such obscure passages of Scripture, though. It is rather based on the sure knowledge that in Christ God has begun a new thing which will one day find its climax in His coming again. Between that first and second coming, however, we are called on to be responsible travelers of the Way, living by faith and not by sight. We do see "signs," of course—signs that the world is returning to its Maker and Judge.

They are not signs that give us a roadmap, though. They are only signs to keep us on the Way. And when the end comes, it shall be as we round an unexpected curve and confront the King of Glory, who will ask only if we have faithfully followed the path given us in Christ.

2

Religion by Unconcealed Power

There is nothing particularly new about speaking of "the end of the world." Christian theology has understood that the world is moving toward its conclusion and judgment ever since Christ promised to return again after the period of His absence initiated by His ascension into the heavens.

The *imminence* of this end has been a prominent theme of the Christian faith, for that matter. Christ's return has never been considered to be far removed from human history. To be sure, there have been times when people seemed far more aware of this nearness of the end than at other times, but always in the background of the faith the certainty of Christ's return has kept Christian people watching for the end of the present world.

This end of the world, of course, has also been understood as the "beginning of a new age," for one can find references from Isaiah through the visions of John in the Book of Revelation of "the new heavens and the new earth." The end, then, was not strictly speaking an end of all things, but rather the end of the fallen age and the beginning of the renewed age. What is seen will be ended in order to give way to a new world, a re-creation by God of an order and age in which His will shall perfectly be seen and done.

What *is* new is the seriousness with which the world as such takes talk about "end times." With the rise of humanistic enterprises, philosophies, and sciences generally divorced from direct interaction with the church, a mind-set of optimistic and hopeful anticipation about the future of the world had set in. Talk about the "end of the world" seemed foreign to this hopeful optimism, and it was replaced by a vocabulary of expectation and anticipation of things yet to come. That mind-set was short-lived, though, ending with the coming of the atomic bomb. Since the end of World War II a progressive deterioration has taken place in this hopeful optimism as waves of ecological fear were coupled with the continued escalation of armaments both in number and in power. Within a decade the secular mind has turned with seriousness to the question of whether mankind will show enough restraint to preserve civilization as we know it much beyond the turn of the century. The fear is that a nuclear holocaust, a genetic development set loose upon the face of the earth, an ecological backlash from our industrial development, or some similar disaster will bring an end to the world that only a few years ago seemed crowned with unhindered promise.

Although it is always somewhat tricky to analyze just why certain movements, religious or otherwise, take root and flourish at some times while they wither at other times, it would appear that the combination of world crises with some of the things we have already discussed in this book has made "religion by unconcealed power" a very popular expression of religion today. A form in which this expression is given shape today is called "millennialism." To understand the concerns we express here, it will be necessary for us to examine at some length (although even then only in a very cursory form) the basic thrust of this expression. It has been most popularly put forth in the best seller by Hal Lindsey called *The Late Great Planet Earth,* but it can be found in many similar books on today's religious bookshelves.

The essential "mix" of millennial thinking revolves around this core:

Since God made great promises to Israel of old, many of which have never come true in a clearly discernible way, some explanation must be made in order to retain the integrity of the Biblical promises. Those promises are basically twofold: (1) Israel will possess the land given to their father Abraham by promise and briefly owned by them from the days of Joshua to the Babylonian captivity. The temple in which God promises to reside with a special presence is closely tied to this promise of the land. (2) God will save Israel, for Israel is a chosen nation, a unique people through whom the glory of God will be seen in all the world.

Since God never reneges on a promise, it is therefore plain that Israel must regain its land and Israel must be saved. These two fulfillments are part of the end-time plan of God according to proponents of this mode of thinking.

The first of those promises has been fulfilled in the restoration of Israel to the Jewish people, supporters of this view tell us. When the Zionist movement of the early part of this century culminated in the Declaration of Independence signed on May 14, 1948, and David Ben-Gurion announced the establishment of a Jewish nation to be known as the State of Israel, the beginning of God's renewal of His

20

mighty activity in behalf of Israel could be detected.

This sets the stage for the second fulfillment of prophecy—the salvation of Israel. Although as a whole Israel has never believed in Jesus, God cannot simply let Israel go its own way. He must act according to His promise. He has not forgotten Israel, nor has He forgotten all the promises He made to that nation.

The long period of rejecting Christ may be explained in various ways, depending on whether one is a "dispensationalist" or not, but in one way or another the restoration of the State of Israel is the first in a series of steps that indicate God's renewed action in behalf of Israel . His ultimate act will be the conversion and salvation of Israel. The whole history of the world will be affected in the train of events leading to this conversion.

The "proof" for this is an intricate web of proof passages drawn at times in willy-nilly fashion from all over the Scriptures. Almost any development of history seems to trigger a new series of passages put together to fit the needs of the situation, showing that it had been predicted. It is held that a sort of ladder of events is being built up by God in "fulfillment" of these "predictions." This school of thought is convinced that events are now working out in the world in accord with past predictions in such a way that God is showing with His mighty power how He can direct the entire course of history to the ends of His own choosing.

This is why we call this "religion by unconcealed power." It perceives God to be using His mighty arm to produce the ends He wills. He is, as it were, singlehandedly directing the entire program of events so that predictions of long ago will literally be fulfilled.

In many of these millennialistic schemes the "rapture" interrupts the course of world events, removing all believers from the scene and leaving only unbelievers in the world.

(A note is undoubtedly in order here, for the reader may be rather confused by now with terms such as "dispensationalist," "millennialist," "rapture," etc. There are many types of schemes we are trying to describe in a brief overview here, and this is neither the time nor place to attempt to sort through the differences between the schemes, much less to attempt to define all the specialized terms that have been developed by the various people who have proposed and devised these systems of thought. We mention them here only to give some hints of directions a person who wants to understand these schemes of thought better might take to get more information. If you can just stay with us a bit longer, some of it may make more sense. We need to catch the broad directions of "religion by

21

unconcealed power" if we are going to see the problems it has raised for more orthodox understandings of the faith.)

This "rapture" is vividly described in words, in drawings, in bumper stickers, and in many other ways as the sudden and abrupt removal of all those who confess the name of Christ. The intention is to pave the way for the reintroduction of God's original plan. Not all systems of thought are willing to put it this way, but the "dispensational" school of belief (very widely held in many millennialist circles today) sees the development of the church, which will end at the rapture, as a sort of detour of God's original plan. Although the original intention was to save Israel through Jesus by restoring it to power among the nations and making of it the great nation promised to Abraham, Israel's rejection of Christ changed God's plan of attack. Jesus turned instead to a preaching of grace and in giving Himself on the cross made salvation available also to the Gentiles. This is the "dispensational" age that will end in the rapture, and the original intention of God will again be taken up—namely, the giving of salvation to Israel.

They, of course, are among the "unbelievers" who will be left at the time of the rapture, since they will not have accepted Christ. That opens the way for God to deal directly with His people in a new way. Although there will be no "believers" left to give witness at this time, presumably written materials and especially volumes of the Scriptures will remain. The main thrust of this conversion activity of God, however, appears to be more a manifestation of His divine power as world events reveal His activity more and more clearly through this time.

When one reads the literature or hears speakers on this subject any number of variations may be heard on what happens in the intervening time between the rapture of the believers and the basic conversion of the Jews, but essentially one hears of two divisions of three and a half years (in total, of course, seven years) of great strife and bloodshed across the faces of Europe, western Asia, and northern Africa. Apparently all other nations have dropped from international significance, for nothing of consequence is tied to any countries other than Europe (as a whole, called the renewed Roman Empire), Russia, China (crossing into the Mid-East in warfare), Israel, and the other nations in the area as they become victimized, so to speak, by this giant mix of hostilities.

The Biblical proof-texting for this enormously detailed blueprint is drawn from almost anywhere an "interpreter" chooses, but the so-called "apocalyptic books" (apocalyptic is a special type of literature that flourished in Israel between 200 B.C. and 100 A.D., of which there is a considerable library of extra-Biblical examples) of Daniel and Revelation provide rich resources for piecing this system of thought together.

The end of this tremendous upsurge of violence and suffering will come when the Antichrist, who has been behind this strife, is subdued and overcome by the return of Christ. At this point Christ will initiate a thousand years' reign ("millennial" means "thousand") in which His peace and prosperity will rule the world through the nation of Israel out of Jerusalem. During this reign the temple will be rebuilt (some variations, many of them popular today, have the temple rebuilt as one of the events triggering the seven years of violence mentioned earlier), the Old Testament system of sacrifices and rituals will be restored, and Israel will enjoy unparalleled material blessings as promised in the Old Testament. Through the missionary activity of the converted Israelites great numbers of people will be won for the Lord.

This thousand-year reign is mentioned only in Revelation 20, but it serves basically as the triggering mechanism by which the whole previously described scheme of events is worked out, using, as mentioned, a set of Bible passages that seem upon closer scrutiny to have been drawn almost without rhyme or reason from many parts of the Bible.

On the strength of the Revelation 20 chapter it is assumed that the thousand years will end with Satan, who has been chained in impotence through this entire period of time, being released again briefly. Then a final battle will end his power once and for all, after which the end of all things will come.

One must never assume that there is any unanimity whatever among those who hold such views of the "end time," nor do we mean to imply this by the brief description just given. There are as many beliefs about the millennium and its surrounding circumstances as there are interpreters, one is led to believe from the literature, for it lends itself beautifully to all sorts of speculative schemes and has great potential for any creative thinker who likes to string Bible passages together in one way or another with imagination.

It is hardly based on sound Biblical interpretation, however. We shall discuss the larger problem of Biblical interpretation in chapter 5, but at this point we need to note some of the problems involved.

In any attempt at Biblical interpretion one must carefully distinguish what is true to the original intention of the Biblical authors and what is mere fanciful dreaming on the part of interpreters. That is never an easy task, and it is more complicated in the case of many who pursue "religion by overt power" precisely because they are so intensely dedicated to the proposition that the Bible is inspired and inerrant and infallible in all its parts from beginning to end. Were they doubters or people who express a desire to "play" with the Word, one could meet the problem head on. But they, like us, receive the Bible as the full testimony of God's will and seek to find in it His blueprint for the future and His plan of action to carry out that blueprint.

God's words and acts are indeed in harmony. No serious student of Scripture or Christian believer will dispute that point. The question is how to determine the intention of God in the words He has spoken through His prophets and evangelists and how to receive them as living words for our own day and time. That is our task.

Many people would say that it is not ours to judge, that every person has a right to his/her own interpretation and we are not to infringe on that right. Better to simply tolerate the exercise of imagination over against the end times, since little harm seems to be done, some may say. One can never argue with people who engage in such endless quests for support of a view they have taken up, it might be continued, so better to let the whole thing alone. Good as that may sound, some things need to be said and seriously considered over against the millennial positions we have attempted to capsulize in the past few pages.

Apart from the fact that such ideas disturb many people who run up against them for the first or even the 50th time (and I have many people ask me about things like this), several points of concern need to be noted for our consideration here. Let them first simply be enumerated, and then we shall spend some time examining them at greater length.

1. The view of history proposed by this school of thought is very close to a "fatalism" that does away with the basic areas of human freedom.

2. This understanding of God's ways among humankind works far more with fear than it does with faith, not withstanding vigorous denials of this assertion when proponents are confronted with it.

3. "Religion by unconcealed power" assumes or at least insinuates that God works more with force and might than He does with grace and love. Thus the primary thrust of the Scriptures is turned from a love seeking to entice creation from its waywardness

24

to a description of how God's powerful drive to get His way will win out in the long run.

4. Scripture is thus remade into a guidebook for the future rather than an unfolding of God's continuing concern for His lost and wandering creation.

5. Ultimately, this way of thinking anticipates a heaven on earth, looking for and hoping for a basic modification of human life under Christ's lordship apart from the transforming qualities of His redemptive work of the cross. The Gospel is thus pushed off center as God's power dominates what God's grace cannot win by the influence of love.

These are serious concerns, and we shall attempt to show how serious they are by a closer examination of them. Each of these problems can be seen independently, but because there is an overlap among them, one also has to view them as a whole.

These charges clearly reveal why we have chosen to speak of these forms of religious expression as "religion by unconcealed power." When one listens for any period of time or reads with any detail the literature of those who are of the millennialist persuasion, it becomes evident rather quickly that for them the most impressive thing about God is the way He makes everything work out the way He wants it. Although there will be a recognition that sin has interrupted God's intention and that Israel's unbelief momentarily diverted His efforts from Israel to the Gentiles, in the long run God will exert His power to make things turn out the way He says they will in spite of these human interruptions of His intention.

On the one hand this makes of prophecy a blueprint for God's action, as we have suggested. Since the nature of prophecy has been discussed at some length in the first chapter, we need not review that material again here. We can see, however, that "religion by unconcealed power" has strong overlap with a variety of other religious expressions popularly held in our day.

The question that is laid bare by this approach to Scripture is primarily this one: Who will be able to decode the prophetic blueprint and be found looking for its fulfillment in the proper way? In other words, to understand prophecy in this way, expecting God's power to do exactly what He predicted in the prophetic Word, is to believe that God tells us ahead of time what He is going to do, that it is our task to figure out what He is going to do, to expect it to happen in just that way, and then to stand under His protection while He makes it happen in exactly that way.

This is what we mean by the charge that this is virtually a "fatalistic" view of the nature of history. Fatalism is a view of history that says we as humans have no power to determine the course of events at all. We are trapped in a scheme of events that happens around us and through us and that will sweep us with the tide to whatever end this chain of events is moving. There is no point in resisting this chain of events. The only course open to us is to simply accept whatever happens, with neither boasting as though we have in some way been involved in bringing it to pass nor whining and complaining about our fate. It is the ultimate form of the "whatever will be, will be" type of mentality.

This type of thinking may extend into the remotest forms of human activity, suggesting that it was foreordained and planned before the foundations of the earth that we were going to draw our pants on, left leg first, at precisely 7:03 a.m. on Tuesday or that we were going to boil an egg at 3:30 p.m. on Sunday afternoon. It sees every earthquake foreordained as well as every ache of our body predetermined outside of any chain of human or universal inter-action of events that could possibly alter what was long ago established.

Although most practitioners of "religion by unconcealed power" do not quite move to the extremes suggested above, one need not read or listen long to their faith systems to find that their basic intention in "searching the Scriptures" is to find out and uncover exactly what it is that God has in store for the world so that they will "know" (notice how different this is from searching the Scriptures as a source of "faith"!) exactly what will happen in just what order of events. This is what we mean by the charge that Scripture is remade into a guidebook for the future. That becomes its primary purpose for those committed to this persuasion. "Faith" is thus transformed into "knowledge."

Once that becomes the primary use for Scripture, the other things are likely to follow.

Human freedom, for example, becomes minimal. About all that is left of it is on an individual level, largely in the area of accepting or not accepting this plan of God for our salvation. This would be true for the present, but one gets the impression that after the seven years of great tribulation faith will be fostered more by the marvelous display of God's power which is irresistible than it will be through anything like the means of grace, the Word and the sacraments. For now, however, there would apparently be this kind of private leeway given for human freedom in that people are called on to confess the name of Jesus or to reject it. For that reason there is usually a strong evangelistic thrust to the proclamation of millennialist groups.

This freedom is largely and almost exclusively in the arena of private faith and ethics, however, for the larger movement of events is generally spoken of as determined by God Himself. It is He who, as it were, "sets up" the scene for the Antichrist (evidently a "foreknown" although not necessarily God-made enemy who is the protegé of Satan and the object of God's great wrath in this "end time" preceding the millennium). It is He who establishes the opposing forces that will struggle against the victory of evil. It is He who returns visibly in the second coming of Christ and eventually conquers. Nations are more pawns than self-willed actors in this giant struggle of Armageddon. There is no significant freedom permitted the world forces whatever, for they all have their places assigned them and God will see to it that His blueprint is filled out according to all the specifications laid down therein.

Although short of fatalism in its most drastic form, this anticipation of the future approaches fatalism to the point where the Scriptures are almost totally remade in terms other than their original intention.

When this plan of the future is placed before people, the first response is commonly one of fear. Many people have spoken to me in just those terms after having read one of these books or seen the various movies portraying the coming time of trouble.

The fear is supposedly balanced by the assurance that those of faith will be "raptured" into heaven before the greatest onslaught of tribulation. That is why these movements are generally characterized by strong evangelistic thrusts, trying to save as many people as possible from these great distresses of the tribulation leading to the beginning of the millennium.

For a variety of reasons, though, the balance rarely comes off well. A friend of mine pointed out one day as we were talking about this, "You can scare hell out of people, but you can't scare heaven into them!" And perhaps that is putting the problem as simply as possible. If fear is the primary result of this kind of teaching and evangelism receives its chief impetus out of scare tactics, the whole effort distorts the Biblical intentions.

Carol had been having some personal difficulties and had been coming to see me off and on for a period of time. Those difficulties probably made her even more susceptible than others may have been to suggestions of the coming time of trouble about which we have been speaking. It was no surprise therefore, when she came into my office one day very much disturbed about the things we have been talking about. A friend had been pointing out how closely her understanding of some of the prophetic passages dovetailed with current events that were headline material. "Pastor, we must surely be living in the end time," she said, her voice quavering with such fear that she could hardly control herself.

I could not disagree with the basic statement, for it is indeed part of our Christian confession that we live in the end time. But I inquired why this should suddenly make her so afraid, since the coming of Christ to judge the quick and the dead is part of our weekly confession of faith in the creeds of the church. I asked further, "Why are you suddenly convinced that Christ is more likely to come tomorrow than in another 1,000 or 1,500 years? Every age has seen signs of His nearness, but why is our age closer to the end than any other age? Or why can't it be put off still again to a later time?"

It was then she told me about the aforementioned conversation. She mentioned a few of the signs her friend had pointed out to her, with the general Scriptural documentation. "Somehow it's like death, I suppose," Carol said. "I know that I'm going to die sometime, but if I knew I was going to die this evening I would think about it differently. Even though I've always believed Christ would return to judge the quick and the dead, as you said, it just sort of threw me into a terror when we were talking about His coming again in such a short time."

Gradually she settled down a bit and recognized that even if He were to come that very day, it would not be a disaster. In a sense, for that matter, the very anticipation of His coming again is the *hope* laid before Christian people of all ages. As we were able to talk about this I pointed out: "The Biblical anticipation of the end time is generally an attempt to raise hope and to sustain faith, not to raise fear or to dampen the spirits of the living! The end times are times for affirmation of faith, times of encouragement toward continued growth and steadfastness and good works."

I pointed out a couple passages in particular like 2 Peter 3:11-13 to show what I meant: "Since all these things are thus to be dissolved, what sort of persons ought you to be in lives of holiness and godliness, waiting for and hastening the coming of the day of God, because of which the heavens will be kindled and dissolved, and the elements will melt with fire! But according to His promise we wait for new heavens and a new earth in which righteousness dwells."

"But don't the Scriptures also have terrible and fearful descriptions of the last days?" Carol remembered some of the passages her friend had pointed out. She remembered especially some sections of Revelation that had frightened her terribly.

"You must recognize first of all that Revelation is a particular kind of writing," I pointed out. "It has a sort of coded language familiar to the readers of John's day, but not particularly familiar to us today. Perhaps we can talk about that at another time.

"For now I'm more interested in the larger intention of the Book of Revelation . . . or of all the New Testament documents, for that matter. They intended to help people understand what it means to live in this final age of the world now set into motion by the coming of Jesus. God had signalled in the Christ that His intentions of love, so long shown to the nation of Israel, were now being extended across the entire face of the earth. Somehow everything that had ever happened to Israel had come together in this Christ, the man known as Jesus of Nazareth. To 'believe' in Him was to share in the love of God that had so long hovered over the earth in and through the people called Israel.

"The intention of the writers, then, was to help people perceive how much God loved the world of His creation, even though it had fallen away from Him and went its own way. The Biblical writers say in many ways, in fact, that those who have always had to fear God and build their religious faith and life on fear can now turn from those ways and find in God a Father of love. That will transform everything about the way they believe and live!"

"Why are all those frightful pictures in the Bible, then?" Carol had been very impressed by the images that are enough to instill fear in the bravest of souls if they are isolated from the texts!

"The images are very real for a reason," I explained. "The early Christians encountered intense persecution very early in their history. Jesus had warned them it would be so . . . and He was right. At first they endured it without too much question, but after several waves of persecution had swept over them you can imagine the questions that were starting to arise among them. It seemed as though this was a strange way for God to be 'blessing' His people! Many started wondering, in fact, if the continued persecutions might be a sign of opposition from God Himself . . . especially since the Roman emperors who were behind the major persecutions had all pronounced themselves gods. It seemed to be turning into a contest of the Roman gods vs. the Christian God, and the Roman gods always seemed to be winning. Why did God remain so silent?

29

Why was there no respite for those who called themselves by the name of Christ?

"Those questions lie behind what I have called 'apocalyptic literature,' the sort you find in Revelation. The fearful images are the pictured destruction of those who oppose God. It's the way of sustaining faith employed by John and other authors when Christian people wanted reassurance. Those authors envisioned the time when God would visibly crush the opposing forces so that all the earth could see. It was, as it were, a way of seeing the present time through the eyes of the future when Christ would return again."

Carol is typical of many people who, when they encounter those pictures of the future, respond with great fright and considerable anxiety. Words originally meant to encourage faith are turned into words that fill people with fear. Pictures designed to portray ultimate victory are turned into words that portray a time of coming tribulation. God's eternal kingship is reduced, at least momentarily, into a thousand years' reign here on earth. Words of promise are turned into words of threat.

Many times, it must be recognized, this happens inadvertently. Those who hold these positions frequently do not *intend* to bring about results like this. General experience shows, though, that fear is a common result and that the message is often perceived more as one of threat that calls for response than it is of love that entices and grace that beckons to us from the Lord of mercy.

Perhaps this is true at least in part because there is frequently something of a mixture between the way God is dealing with us now and the way He will deal in the millennial period. Following the terrible fearfulness of the seven years of tribulation during which the display of His might will call some people to faith (remember that all the former believers are now gone because of the rapture), the very presence of Christ as ruler through the thousand years will make it hard *not* to believe! After all, how can one deny that which is apparent to all who can see when Christ reigns personally?!

Thus there will be no more need for the means God has presently placed at our disposal as His ties to us—the Word, our Baptism, the Holy Supper. Why should one use them when Christ is directly accessible? So, according to this scheme, we will no longer walk by faith but by sight.

If we shall live by sight in the future, the sight is already pursued in the present by attempts to "decode" the Scriptures in order to obtain God's blueprint for what will yet come to pass. Once that blueprint is available, we merely need to sit by and watch God

30

unfurl His power to make things work out as He has told us they would. Thus His power is the mainspring for all that we call faith, and faith is primarily necessary so that believers can say sometime in the future, "See, I told you it would be like this!"

The eventual end of all this, then, is a reign of Christ on this earth in which His power shall enforce His will. The thousand-year reign projected by many who propose a "religion by unconcealed power" has little or nothing to do with Jesus' *cross*. It is, to be sure, the *resurrected* Christ who reigns, but the resurrection is itself primarily a display of unconcealed power rather than an affirmation of the hidden power that lies deeply imbedded in His voluntary giving of self into death. The power of the cross is very different from the visible power envisioned in the glory revealed in the thousand years of earthly reign anticipated by those who are anxious to have their faith affirmed by sight and knowledge and proof, worked out among the kingdoms of this world.

Such hopes see the transformation of this world coming about by virtue of Christ's lordship and the power He can exercise in the personal reign He will exercise over the earth. This hope is in radical contrast to the hope of the church expressed through the ages—the transformation of the world through the quiet grace exercised in the hearts of men and women through the indwelling of the Holy Spirit who comes through Word and sacrament. Hoping for Christ's appearance in power and glory to reign on earth is very different from the faith and confidence that Christ is even now present and ruling, although His rule remains hidden under the veil of His grace that calls men and women to repentance and faithful living even while the earth continues its stubbornly erring way.

This is not to deny His power. Nor is it to say that His power will never be displayed. It is only to deny that life as we experience it in sin will be interrupted with such a display of power that sin will be overcome in and by that power. Sin is, in a sense, a power in itself that has overcome us and has stolen our will from its true and proper Master.

Christ overcame sin through the weakness of the cross, through the submission of His sinless life to the will of the Father who gave Him as the Man for all humanity. Sin was surprised in this, that whereas it prepared to defend itself on the grounds of power, it was overcome in the humility and weakness of the cross. It is to this kind of weakness that we are called, that sin might be overcome. We are called to humility, to faith, to quiet submission to the will of the Father. In this God's power is made perfect—in our weakness!

31

This is the problem that lies at the root of "religion by overt power." It keeps its eye on the returning and victorious Christ without understanding the place of weakness and faith in the middle of the world's suffering. It wants and anticipates glory without enduring the suffering of the cross. It hopes for resurrection without giving proper place to the dying-ness of the world. This is what we mean when we assert that it pushes the Gospel off its central position in Christian thinking, replacing it with a hope centered in God's overt power.

These are hard words to say to people who are so deeply committed to seeing in the Bible the Word of God. They are not meant unkindly. They are meant as a corrective to abuses that all too often lead to fear rather than to faith, to Bible study as a search for the future rather than an unfolding of the story of God's ongoing concern that His wandering and lost creation return home again.

Two closing remarks should still be made.

Millennialism, which has been the primary focus of this chapter although there are some other similar manifestations of "religion by overt power," is by no means new to the Christian scene. It has been held in various forms since the very earliest days of the church—at least partly because there were forms of it already present in Judaism, from which Christianity sprang. A number of early church fathers held varieties of millennial beliefs. The reader can well imagine how this type of thinking flourished around the turn of the millennium as the year 1000 A.D. neared! Some of the people Luther had to most strenuously resist were millennialists.

It never became a part of nor acceptable to the mainstream of Christian thought, however. Some of the reasons for this are dealt with in this chapter, for millennial thought is again having a strong hearing in our day. Other reasons have to do with the very nature of Biblical interpretation, which will be taken up in chapter 5.

The second thing we need to note in closing is that we have taken issue primarily with what is known as *pre*millennialism in this chapter. There are still other varieties of millennialism that have been in vogue at other times in the history of the church. In fact, the particular type of premillennial view held most widely in our day was basically never proposed before the early part of the 19th century. So while it must be recognized that millennialism as such has been held in various forms by peripheral groups throughout the history of the church, even though discredited in the mainstream of the church's teaching, the type of millennial thinking put forth in most instances today is a new and different kind of thinking from that held earlier. It therefore requires some special consideration. Since the other forms of millennialism are not particularly popular in our day, we have chosen not to spend any time or space in examining these variants of "religion by unconcealed power" that have been popular in prior ages.

3
Religion by Signs

Bill, a pre-med student applying at several medical schools for admission, had been invited by a friend to attend a "prayer meeting" to be held in a house across town. He did not know whether he should go or not, and stopped by to talk with me about it. A little circle of people had invited a traveling evangelist to have services with them for the week, and they were reporting miraculous healings. That was what disturbed Bill. He was willing to accept his friend's invitation to join in prayer with fellow Christians, but whether he wanted to get involved with "healing services" he was not sure.

"My friend told me that he saw a miracle take place right before his eyes," Bill said. "He told me of a fellow who had been born with one leg shorter than the other. He had worn a built-up shoe on one foot all his life. Everybody knew that. Then, last night, they prayed over him and his leg got longer. His limp had changed the other way . . . he limped because his built-up shoe made *that* leg too long now! That's what Jack told me!"

I had to admit that would amaze me, too, although I admitted with Bill that I was a bit skeptical about whether things happened just in that way. Neither of us could challenge Jack's claim, of course, since we had not been there. "How does that make you afraid about going to the meeting this evening, though?" I queried. "Do you mean that you're afraid you won't feel dcomfortable with the evangelist or that he'll call for some decision on your part? What frightens you about going tonight?"

"Jack told me that others were going to be there for prayer, hoping for healing, again this evening. I guess the things you mentioned are all part of it, but frankly, I don't know how I might respond if some special 'miracle' like we've been talking about would take place right before my eyes!" Bill didn't like to offend his friend, but he plainly was disturbed at the prospect of going along that evening.

34

I knew what he was talking about. I had been in a position not too different a couple years earlier. I remembered thinking to myself what a huge amount of explaining I was going to have to do to myself if I actually saw something "supermiraculous" happen right before my eyes. When someone claims to have been cured of ulcers or cancer, one can always say to oneself, "He only *thinks* he has been cured. He will have to face up to his illness again in a few days, but for now he at least has the momentary peace of thinking he has been cured." One does not have to seriously wrestle with the question of whether there has actually been a healing or of what that means.

When one sees a crippled arm healed on the spot or a festering sore disappear or a leg lengthen before one's eyes, though—what then? Many people claim actually to have seen healings like that. I remember my fear, similar to Bill's, when I was present in a situation where at least the possibility of such a miracle was requested in prayer over an afflicted person. For whatever reason, I was spared the need to ask myself such questions, for no healings took place when I was present.

To this day my ears have heard many such reports, but my eyes have never seen such things happen in this "supermiraculous" way as they have been described. So I had retained some of my skepticism about whether things happened just as described when Bill was asking me what I thought about his going to the meeting that evening. I parried with him a bit:

"I would imagine you'd be most happy to see such a healing, wouldn't you?"

Bill saw through me immediately, though. "You know it isn't as simple as that. Of course I would be glad for any relief of suffering, but the question is deeper than that. I don't know how to put it, but I just don't feel comfortable putting my faith on the line like that."

Bill had a proper intuition, for he was trying to say that he didn't want to make his faith dependent on signs, and this was the sort of situation in which signs and faith were very closely tied together. If he saw some "supersign," would that mean that God had been especially gracious at this one point in life or would it—*should* it—be broadened to mean that any faith "worth its salt" will somehow be related to healing? I encouraged Bill to go if he could at all feel comfortable with such a decision, for although one should not unduly place faith into jeopardy by exposing it unnecessarily to doubts, it is also true that faith cannot be protected so much that it becomes a "hothouse faith." He had not been invited to a setting alien to or opposed to Christian faith, even though it was not the way in which he ordinarily had heard and seen that faith expressed and confessed.

That, of course, is much of what disturbs people when confronted with situations like this. They do not feel comfortable, on the one hand, with what seems to be an undue stress on the search for signs of the power of faith. Yet those who are involved in such activity are committed to the confidence that God acts according to His promise. How does one sort through such difficult questions?

Is there a place for "signs" in confessing Christian faith? If the healing of people from earthly diseases or speaking in tongues or some other designated sign is to be *the* sign of faith or even *a* sign of *greater* faith, that is quite foreign to the main thrust of Christian understanding throughout the ages. Yet Christians have never been afraid to speak of many "signs" of faith's deeper realities, whether it be the very existence of the created world around us or the occurrence of unusual events in the history of Israel or the resurrection of Christ from the dead. When people who want to live by faith step past a faith grounded in the words of faith we believe to have been inspired in the Scriptures and as enfleshed in Christ and seek present reassurances through continuing miraculous signs of one sort or another, we rightfully get rather edgy about the nature of that faith.

It is true that many so-called "healings" are hardly flukes or false reports. One of my parishioners had planned for surgery, had the hospital room reserved, and was having her final checkup by her doctor preparatory to entering the hospital when her doctor gave her the good news that she did not have to undergo surgery, for the tumerous growth had subsided and was no longer present. She had expressed her fears to me and had told me of the urgency of her prayers. The good news of her recovery was beyond explanation by anybody. It could only be termed miraculous. Nearly everyone knows of at least one or two such marvelous "recoveries" or "healings."

Yet for every situation like that one finds many more examples of the opposite. With equal urgency of prayer the tumor remains, the difficulty increases, crippling and death come in spite of faith. One can never deny the *possibility* of miraculous healings, but one dare never rely on the *probability* of such healings. Is that a sign of lack of faith? Hardly!

All who call themselves by the name of the Risen One, Jesus Christ, most certainly will affirm that God *can* perform miracles in our day no less than in Biblical times. His past record speaks for

36

itself in the Bible, for He has acted in the most unexpected ways at the most unexpected places at the most unexpected times! That is part of the faith confessed by anyone who takes the Bible seriously. The question is not whether He *has* done such things or whether He *can* do such things.

The question, rather, is whether we can, in a manner of speaking, control when and where He will do such things so that they are responses to our faith or our urgent prayer or in some ways "signs" of His presence as we attempt to affirm it by our own actions. When is our faith and prayer and expectation properly expressed and at what point do we tempt Him to prove His presence by irrefutable signs? It is true that we too frequently "do not have because we do not ask," as James puts it (James 4:2). But can we turn our prayers into demands when we pray with too much emphasis on how, when, and where the prayer is to be answered? Can we require signs that God has not promised to give? These are the crucial questions that lie at the heart of our concerns when we speak of "religion by signs."

Such questions were raised most forcibly for me one time when I attended such a meeting at the invitation of a fellow who was hosting such a "healer."

A husband explained the absence of his wife by telling of how, in spite of some medication given her for a nervous breakdown a short time before this, she simply was not feeling well enough to attend this meeting. She had apparently been there one or two nights previously, for the group, including the visiting evangelist, seemed to know her. It was suggested that they pray over the husband by proxy since he and his wife were "one flesh," asking for healing in the wife. This they did with great fervency and the laying on of hands on the husband in behalf of his wife.

Following this prayer the evangelist advised the husband to go home and throw all her medication down the drain. If I remember correctly, in fact, he called the medication "tools of the devil" and continued reliance on them an act of unbelief. At the least it was suggested in one way or another that to have kept the medications would indicate a lack of faith.

I hope this was an extreme example, although my under-standing is that this approach is used far more widely than I would like to believe. To say the least, this violates all the limitations of prayer as intercession in behalf of the needy one, making it a demand that God must meet in response to our faith.

Therein lies the kernel of "heresy" when religion requires signs from God. If prayer or faith is made the healing agent, one has made prayer largely a mode of "positive thinking," in which so many people lay great stock. If we only think right or believe right about things, they say, then things will turn out all right. But as you well know, it is pure nonsense to believe earnestly that putting my finger into a live socket will not shock me. There are many things about life that are true whether we believe them or will them or not. The sun rises whether we will it to or not—or even whether we believe it will or not. Many things—*most* things, for that matter—about life are beyond the range of our will or our capacity to control by believing.

Sickness and disease lie somewhere in the shadowy "between" areas of life, interestingly enough. We know there are many "psychosomatic illnesses" that are largely the result of and are subject to our subconscious, unconscious, and conscious will. We also know that in some of the Eastern religions it has been clearly demonstrated that humans have extraordinary possibilities of controlling everything from blood flow through respiratory activity without undue harm to bodily existence. Such exercises have been shown, in fact, to be available to us without too much extraordinary effort, and biofeedback is one of the big areas of research and even treatment in today's medical practices. Health is seen today in a "wholistic" way far more than it was a few years ago.

Yet sickness and disease are plainly not entirely in the hands of our own willing, either. We are subject to forces outside our control that exercise ultimate mastery over us. Our best efforts result in remarkable results, but those best efforts are in their turn subject to another.

The question returns to us more complicated than we first asked it, then. When and where can we speak of healing as a "sign" from God? Perhaps some who call themselves "healers" are only masters at bringing to the surface and making it possible to overcome those subconscious, unconscious, and on occasion even conscious causes of human affliction. That would not particularly be a "sign from God" but would rather indicate the latitude we have in our human existence to control what happens among us. Perhaps some people exercise such faith in the healers themselves that they overcome the inner compulsions that have incapacitated them with the conviction that special power lies in the healer when, in fact, the healer only triggered mechanisms within the person him/herself that relieved the problem. It is difficult to determine what makes some healers successful while others attempt such activity with little or no real success whatever.

38

However one explains this, it is all a far cry from Christian faith and its understanding of prayer. Far different from "positive thinking" or the relief of psychosomatic symptoms, Christian faith looks to God as the one in whom all these forces are held together and to whom they must ultimately pay obedience. When people accuse someone of having too little faith and thereby explain why healing did not take place, faith is made the agent of healing rather than God Himself. Faith or prayer takes on its meaning only as it looks to and submits itself to God. It is God who heals. It is God in whom we believe. It is to God that we pray. Our prayers and our faith are statements of confidence and petitions for mercy directed to a God who looks after His children. We speak as obedient and trusting children filled with trust and confidence that He not only will hear but will respond.

His response, however, is ultimately His own. It cannot be directed by our wishes nor commanded by our faith. God's response to prayer will not be boxed in by our prescriptions of how, when, or where the response should be made. Any suggestion that we should expect a given kind of response at a given time (such as throwing away medication prescribed for a nervous breakdown) is an act of presumption on our part and amounts to putting God on trial as to whether He can produce the results we call for or not.

A fellow in a recent instruction class, Tony by name, raised some serious questions about this when we considered the nature of prayer. He had been raised in a family where medicine was rarely used and prayer was seen as basic to any healing processes. He was by no means just being quarrelsome but brought Biblical questions directly into play. "What do you do, then," he said, "with such passages as when Jesus tells people who have been healed by Him, 'Your faith has made you well'?"

I had to admit that such questions are troublesome, for such passages are by no means uncommon in Scripture. "Still," I said, "I don't really see them as contradicting what has been said, even though on the surface they certainly appear to do so. It is Jesus' way of saying that He respects a faith that brought someone to the right person to deal with the problem at hand. He commends those who bring their troubles straightforwardly and openly to the source of what they are confident is their only help."

Tony scratched his head. "Well . . . maybe! But I wonder if that's not skirting the issue just a bit."

"Think about the times, then, when people wanted to honor the apostles and evangelists for their acts of healing. The Book of Acts has a number of such examples. Every time this came up they quickly denied having any power in themselves. It was not their prayers or their faith that did the mighty deeds. They were quick to assert this, even though both prayers and faith were certainly in use. It was the power of God at work in and through them that made such acts possible. They refused to take honor, but immediately gave it to God, to whom their prayers were sent and in whom they trusted."

There I had trapped myself just when I thought I was home free. It was as if Tony had been waiting for me to say this, for he had had considerable contact with groups in which healing was prominently called for. "If the apostles could do it by the power of God, why can't we?"

I rather lamely gave the usual arguments put forth about how such mighty acts were necessary to establish the early church, but after one or two generations of such activity and a firm rooting of the church such gifts dropped away from general use.

It didn't satisfy him. He kept going back to the question of why it still seemed possible after Jesus was gone and then disappeared. God surely had not become impotent after a generation or two. Why should not such signs of His presence and power be maintained?

These questions are not easily dealt with—at least not in a satisfactory manner. They have lain in the background of Christian faith through most of the history of the church. Yet they are not entirely beyond the interest and concern of Scripture itself.

I reminded Tony of Simon Magus, who wanted to purchase the miracle-working secret and was rebuffed precisely because he mis-interpreted the point of the signs. The apostles and evangelists from the earliest history of the church after Christ's ascension were concerned that they *not* be known primarily as miracle-workers, but as proclaimers of the Gospel.

One cannot say that the early church grew primarily because there were signs accompanying the proclamation of the Gospel. Rather, it was by virtue of the Spirit's blessing upon the proclaimed Word as enacted in the daily life of those first followers of the Christ that the church gained in name and numbers. It is true that wonders and signs are mentioned in Acts 2 during the days immediately following Pentecost, but the emphasis lies elsewhere: "And all who believed were together and had all things in common; and they sold their possessions and goods and distributed them to all, as any had need. And day by day, attending the temple together and breaking bread in their homes, they partook of food with glad and generous

40

hearts, praising God and having favor with all the people. And the Lord added to their number day by day those who were being saved" (Acts 2:44-47). The signs were almost incidental, and nowhere do we read that villages or whole regions were touched by miracles so that all the ill were healed, the hungry fed, and such like. Not even Jesus performed miracles in such a wholesale fashion, even though He had the full disposal of the power of God at His fingertips.

If Jesus Himself, then, used miracles largely to broaden the vision of what the Gospel was about and to help people see what was meant by the drawing near of the kingdom of God, by what right do we lay emphasis upon such signs as the way by which faith is made public and revealed?

Is not our modern counterpart to such activity primarily the enacting of love among the needy? God's presence among us is signaled more by the "everyday miracle of love" than by the "supersigns" of healing and miraculous interventions breaking into our daily afflictions. Is it not true that when we feed the hungry, give drink to the thirsty, and visit the sick and imprisoned in the name of the Christ we give every bit as important and powerful a sign of His presence as He ever asked of us? If ours is an ordinary means of feeding the hungry rather than the multiplication of five loaves of bread and a couple of fish, is it less a miracle of God's presence among us? Or, to carry it a bit further, if medicine and surgery and nutrition and even hygiene and cleanliness are modes of restoring health, rather than the touching of an ear or a command to a lame man that he should walk, is it the time element or the healing itself that is the miracle? Surely we who enliven the Word of God in our daily life of love are the miracles, the signs of God's presence and concern to a world that is mired in its finite limitations.

It is not our faith, but God who has given us the faith, that does such things. Yet the faith indeed lies open to the God who promises to be among us. When He heals my parishioner before she enters the hospital, we praise Him. When He lets another parishioner suffer over a long time, we trust in His compassion even though we cry out with the pain of a moment in which His compassion seems so foreign. Faith is to believe that He cares and that He can and does intervene at unexpected places in unexpected ways, but it is not to define those places and ways. Only God can decide those things.

I was discussing this one day with a woman from my congregation. I was expressing special concern about such acts as described earlier—throwing out necessary medication on the basis of "faith." She was appalled when I told her about it. "Don't they realize what they're doing? Surely they know they'll have to get medication again or return to the doctor again, don't they? How can they keep on believing like that? Aren't they brought to reality sooner or later?"

"Interestingly enough, they've made their own way out of that dilemma without any problem. A little thought will show you how they would respond," I answered.

She said she would never be able to believe again if that sort of thing would happen to her. "Consider your alternatives," I said. "If you receive the sign of healing, your faith has been proved. But if you're not privileged with healing . . . what is the problem?"

"You just haven't believed strongly enough?" she answered a bit hesitantly.

"Of course! Either way . . . whether healing takes place or whether it does not . . . you can fall back on the same argument! If healed, your faith was in a sense 'rewarded.' If you were not healed, the problem is yours . . . not God's. You just didn't believe strongly enough. The solution, then, is to believe more fully and you'll see the 'sign' that faith has its own 'reward.' But there you also see the deep problem with a 'religion by signs,' don't you?

"Without a sign you're dangerously close to unbelief! If you can't show 'evidence' of faith with a 'sign,' you're giving evidence of the opposite, for you're showing that you don't really believe very strongly at all."

Although speaking in tongues is not always tied directly to such healing "signs," one finds them at least loosely associated in many cases. Whether tied together or not, though, the danger in pressing for a manifestation of the Spirit's presence by seeking a gift of "tongues" lies in this same direction.

One must be cautious in making accusations in areas like this, of course. Tongues are frequently spoken of as coming upon people without their having been sought. Many tongues-speaking people will go so far as to play down their gift, properly recognizing it as only one of many possible gifts that may come from the Spirit.

As is the case with healing, so also the gift of tongues is spoken of as a manifestation of the Spirit in the early church. Although mentioned in a number of places, the most extended treatment of the subject is given by Paul in 1 Corinthians 12—14. The fact, however, that Paul had to deal with it at such great length, especially over against the church in Corinth, indicates the dangers of over-emphasizing the gift.

42

Never once did Paul deny it as a gift from the Holy Spirit visited upon some people.

Never once did Paul assert that it was a gift that all people of faith would or should have.

Never once did Paul recognize it as a gift of any greater importance than other gifts, and the assertion to the contrary is more nearly true, that it is a rather minor gift compared to the major gift of love (1 Cor. 13).

One must recognize that Paul himself admits the gift as one the Spirit had given to him, although he never spoke of it in any boastful way. He seems to expect the Spirit to continue giving this and like gifts in the future, so it is hard to argue that such gifts were assumed to be only first century A.D. gifts. Forms of ecstatic utterances are found recognized throughout Old Testament history, and there is no sign that they were thought of as now terminating.

All that being recognized, however, they are never seen as signs either of the presence of faith as such or as a mark of "strong" or "special" faith. They are simply part of the larger body of gifts given by the Spirit at various times in various ways to various people in the interest of serving the larger and overall good of the church.

A "charismatic" person (a term sometimes applied to tongues-speaking people, although it can and should be used in a much larger sense of the term) once explained the resurgence of this gift to me somewhat as follows:

"While speaking in tongues has indeed had an ebb and flow in the history of the church, it has tended to recur and become very visible at critical junctures in the life of the church. Such times seem to call for some sort of divine sign that God remains present and active in the critical moment as a reassurance to the faith of God's people.

"The church is presently in crisis as it has been largely disregarded and its teachings held at arm's length by the increasingly technological and self-dependent world of the late 20th century. Faith is at something of a critical juncture in a world looking for evidence and depending on research to uncover knowledge. So once again signs have reappeared in the form of the ecstatic tongues that defy human understanding. Through them God is giving evidence of His nearness and His power."

Scripture, however, makes it clear that signs have their limitations, to say the least. When the rich man who had ignored and despised Lazarus asked that a "sign" be given to his brothers remaining alive so that they might come to faith and be spared the torment he was enduring, Abraham replied: "They have Moses and the prophets; let them hear them." The rich man did not consider this a strong enough sign to convince his brothers. He wanted something stronger and more vivid . . . like the return of Lazarus, who would appear at their door and tell them of their need for repentance. "If some one goes to them from the dead, they will repent." Abraham insists that signs will do no good if they are set on rejecting the Word of life. "If they do not hear Moses and the prophets, neither will they be convinced if some one should rise from the dead" (Luke 16:19-31).

In something of the same fashion we need to recognize that "religion by signs" confronts the same dilemma. If the Word of the Lord will not be heard, any sign that accompanies it can be and will be explained away by the very people who theoretically will be moved by the "signs" to believe.

As noted earlier, this is not to say that all healings or all utterances of an ecstatic nature are fake or demonic or ungodly. Whatever God sets out to do, He will do—and we cannot deny Him the doing of His will.

To tie faith to the signs, though, is the problem! This certainly is what lies at the heart of Paul's concerns in 1 Cor. 12—14. He recognizes that a variety of gifts were available to the church in Corinth, including the gifts of healing and of tongues. The key to their use, however, is given in 1 Cor. 12:7: "To each is given the manifestation of the Spirit for the common good." If and when such gifts become divisive among believers, they have lost their value. Only when they serve the common good in the name of the Christ are they truly serving their proper intent. All such gifts must add to the confession that "Jesus is Lord" in order to be affirmed by the Christian community. (1 Cor. 12:3). There are many manifestations of the Spirit which serve the purpose that such a confession may be made, and Paul is glad to have any or all of them enhancing the body of Christ. That is very different, though, from making them evidence of faith. They are side-products of the faith, but faith has many side-products, including love and hope and patience. So one is concerned about the presence of faith, but one does not attempt to dictate what side-products will result from its presence.

It is admittedly true that the divisiveness does not always rise from those who have the gifts of the Spirit. Sometimes out of envy, sometimes out of ignorance, and most frequently out of misunderstanding, people who are gifted in ways almost so "ordinary" that they are not perceived as gifts object to the manifestation of special

44

gifts. The divisiveness then arises from those who would block the use of extraordinary gifts of the Spirit in the church. Of this we must be most cautious.

The wariness has arisen, though, from some extremely strong suggestions that unless faith is accompanied by certain types or kinds of signs, it is not present in its fullest forms. When such implications arise, whether implicitly or explicitly, the church must decidedly say that faith can be and is indeed present even apart from such extraordinary signs as are spoken of by charismatic and other groups. While the fulness of the Spirit's gifts must be recognized and used in the church, those gifts should always be found in use to promote the confession that "Jesus is Lord" and in service to the unity of the life of the church.

Instead of a "religion by signs," then, the "signs" are nothing more than part of the much larger witness of the church to the grace and mercy of a God who visits His earth in many ways and who has manifested His presence above all in the form of His Son crucified and risen from the dead.

A most touching testimonial to this power of the Spirit came from the widow of a former parishioner who stood with me at the grave site of her husband. I remembered our discussions about the "charismatic" manifestations of the Spirit long ago. He had openly admitted that he longed for these special gifts. He was a deeply consecrated man and had been told of how much more intensely the presence of the Spirit was felt on the part of those who had received the special gifts. It was more than idle curiosity that led him to want the gifts. He earnestly wanted a closer walk with God.

He had told me that he feared them only on one level . . . he was afraid they might raise in him a pride, a sense of superiority over those who had never received such gifts. So while he prayed earnestly for the gifts, he prayed equally earnestly for a sense of humility that would help him receive them as gifts to be used in service to the body of Christ rather than as signs of privilege that might lead him to pride. He had joined a group of charismatic people in a weekly house meeting and had been prayed over with the laying on of hands many times.

But he had never, to the very end of his life, received any of the gifts that others in the group claimed for themselves.

None of this was mentioned at the grave, but his widow and I visited together later and remembered the life of this fine man. Instead she told me of how beloved he had been . . . always helpful to her and supportive of her through some very difficult times. She told

45

me of his intense activity in the community and of his love for children (they had never had any of their own) that led to his activity in so many community projects for young people. She spoke of how his employer had made a special trip to her home several days after the funeral to tell her how much he had valued her husband and to bring a special gift from his fellow employees. And, of course, she did not have to tell me of his deep involvement in the church, for I had known him on that level very well.

While she was narrating all this, though, I had to think again of his anxious longing for the special gifts of the Spirit and his participation in the charismatic group. Never had he received a "sign" of the sort they all rejoiced to have . . . and yet I had never known a man who was more a "sign" to the world of the presence of God than this man. He had never been bitter about failure to receive the special gifts. He had just wanted a still deeper faith and closer walk with God.

But how could it have been much closer than what was now being described to me by his widow, I thought to myself. He spoke now in tongues none of us could understand in the heavenly mansions, I was sure. But that was all possible because the Spirit had blessed him with such quiet gifts while he was here on earth that hardly anybody thought of them as gifts at all. They were noticed primarily by the void he left when they were no longer visibly employed in the family and community. During his lifetime they had just been taken for granted.

Yet he was one of the most gifted men I had known, and he was now seeing "signs" that would have been unthinkable to him during his earthly life. I wanted so much to ask him if it mattered anymore that he had not received what he earnestly desired. But I knew the answer even though I could not ask the question. For the greatest sign, the one that endures forever, as Paul told the Corinthians, was now the mark of all his living . . . the sign of love!

4

Religion by Decision

Versions of the following conversation can be heard almost daily:

"I'm not sure whether I'm a Christian or not."

"Why do you question it?"

"A friend recently asked me when I had made my 'decision for Christ.' I've always considered myself a Christian. I've grown up in the church and been faithful in attending church and Bible classes. But my friend insists that I cannot be a Christian if I can't speak of a particular time of critical decision for or against Him. I don't ever remember making a decision for Him. I never really thought about it that way at all. But now I wonder if I'm really a Christian or if I've just been playing religious games all my life."

That conversation may take place in a pastor's office, with a Christian friend, or in a share group. It is so ordinary that it is almost commonplace. Yet imbedded in the conversation are a number of problems that need to be faced up to and which we want to look at more closely in this chapter. For common as it is to speak of "religion by decision," the forms in which it is generally spoken of today are relatively new to the religious scene even though there are traces of that kind of question all through the Bible. How does it pose problems in the forms with which it is encountered today? To what extent is it tied to some of the Biblical questions? These are the two poles around which we wish to work as we consider "religion by decision."

I was encountered in an airport with a question like that which opened the discussion above: "Are you a Christian?"

Withou hesitation I responded affirmatively. The next question followed as surely as night follows day: "When did you make your decision for Christ?" My response was rather simple: "I never did. Christ made His decision for me. Or, to put it still better, the Holy Spirit called me in my baptism."

Since it was a somewhat unexpected response, there was a

momentary silence on the part of my questioner. He recovered quickly enough, as anyone knows who has been encountered in this way. "But when did you 'experience Christ'?" he pursued.

"What do you mean by that?"

"When did you really know that Christ was your Lord and Savior? When did you give your heart to Him?"

"I find that something of a strange question," I responded. "If *He* claimed *my* heart through the sending of the Holy Spirit, how can *I* say that *I* decided to receive *Him*? I know that I belong to Him. That's enough for me."

"Well, how do you *know* you belong to Him?" he persisted. On the one hand I could see that he wasn't satisfied with the answer at all, but I could see on the other hand that he was curious by this time because he had evidently never run into quite this line of thought before.

"I've already told you. My baptism is my confidence."

"But that's just water poured on you. Had you decided for Christ when you were baptized?"

"I don't know that I had. I really can't remember, for I was a small baby."

"Then you have *not* made a decision for Christ," he insisted.

"I told you I had not. I said the Holy Spirit called me . . . and that's what my baptism is all about. *You* say that it was just water poured on me. I want to point out that it was water poured on me coupled with the word of Christ's command and promise, 'I baptize you in the name of the Father and of the Son and of the Holy Spirit.' Those are the words of life which make the water a seal of salvation, the promise of God offered to me through the stuff of this world— plain, simple water!"

"That doesn't make sense to me at all. You need to experience Christ to be saved, and you keep side-stepping that."

The conversation went in circles, of course, for baptism was nothing more than a sign of my faith to the young fellow who had initiated the discussion. He simply could not understand how baptism could be related to any "experience of Christ," for he perceived it primarily as a human act, and an act of response at that. For me it was/is an act of faithfulness, an opening of our human scene to the grace of God, an initiation into life with God by virtue of the promise He has placed over against water used in this way.

I did try to press my young friend in the airport to describe this "experience" he insisted everyone must have. He identified it, as most people who speak in these terms will, in terms of precise time and place. He said it was like a cool breeze blowing over him when he finally let himself go and turned his life over entirely to Jesus.

That sort of description is typical of "religion by decision." It has many variations, of course, but always it has in it something of a remembrance of the life before conversion being dominated by anything from deep worries through great sin, a sense of self-release into the hands of a power greater than ourselves, and some sort of refreshing sense of well-being that follows this self-release.

What is different about that from a person who has grown up trusting in this power greater than ourselves, however? Can there not be an equal awareness of peace and joy that resides with one on a steadily increasing basis? Why must this happen all at once or in some definable way or at a describable moment? These are the questions that lie beneath the problems with which this chapter is attempting to deal.

What lies at issue in many of the discussions such as the one described above is a very old question about the relationship between our dependence on God's grace alone for salvation and the need for our human reception of that grace. In other words, it is a common Christian confession that we are saved by grace alone, without the addition of any human works to supplement God's grace. Yet when that grace is offered, there is some kind of human dimension that enters the picture in the form of our "receiving" that grace. How does one describe this receptive posture from our side of the transaction that finally results in what we call "faith"?

Scripture itself recognizes the need for personal commitment to God. The New Testament is filled with such admonitions and exhortations, although they are found in plentiful number in the Old Testament also. The Book of Acts has many urgent calls to faith as it speaks of the early discipling of the world. "Believe in the Lord Jesus and you will be saved," as Paul exhorts the jailer at Philippi in Acts 16:31, is typical of many such Biblical calls to commitment and faith.

With equal intensity, though, the Scriptures assert that grace is entirely a gift of God and that we can do nothing but receive it. "For by grace you have been saved through faith; and this is not your own doing, it is the gift of God—not because of works, lest any man should boast" (Eph. 2:8-9).

Undoubtedly the key phrase which sets up the tensions lying behind the questions of this chapter is to be found in the latter part of the passage just quoted, "Lest any man should boast." When we recognize that we as humans must receive God's gift, our reception

49

dare never become an occasion for boasting. It must always remain a humbling thing to us to recognize that God's grace is a *given* thing, not something we sought out on our own. It was present for us long *before* we knew we needed it or wanted it. It always *precedes* our action, however one can describe our action in receiving it.

That kind of safeguard is undoubtedly necessary, for there is a constant temptation to assume there must be a *reason* for God's giving of grace to those so blessed. It doesn't seem quite right that God would give it in a sort of random way. To put it plainly, "Why does He give it to some and not to others?" That question raises the temptation to answer it, and in answering it we are prone to come up with answers like these:

He gives grace to those whose insight is keen enough to recognize how drastically they need it.

He gives grace to those whose hearts are open to His gifts.

He gives grace to those who have not hardened their hearts against Him and are willing to serve Him.

He gives grace to those whom He sees as being at least potentially better than others . . . or at least not as bad as some people are.

The last-named of these suggested "answers" begins to show very clearly and blatantly what lies beneath all the answers—attempts at explaining the gift of grace in terms of our own works and/or worthiness! Grace freely given can never be explained . . . it can only be received with humility and gratefulness. It is when one attempts to explain the rationale behind the giving, when one tries to understand why grace is given in some situations and not in others, that one gets into theological troubles.

Since our hearts and heads are both very badly infected with sin, we must watch closely these efforts of our reason to understand how grace from God works among us. We are all too prone to subtle forms of work-righteousness and self-justification when we try to explain more than has been revealed to us.

For that reason major segments of Christendom have shied very much from "religion by decision," for the temptations to explain grace lie in that direction. Grace is too easily tied to *our* decision making, to *our* pious experiences, to *our* response at the expense of God's initiating love that lies behind all that we can say about our salvation.

One must recognize, of course, that whole denominations have sprung up around forms of "religion by decision." Altar calls are plain statements of such "invitations to faith" that require personal decision. In some churches one cannot be baptized without some form of identifiable "decision" or "experience of Christ." One does not lightly overlook such major denominational manifestations of "religion by decision" when one warns against such forms of religious expression. Such incorporations of this type of religious understanding into denominational form show that it finds many responsive chords among people who confess the Christian faith.

Yet a word of warning needs to be expressed, for our human inclination is to replace the centrality of God's grace with subtle forms of our own assertions of merit. We walk a very slippery path at points like this.

Tom, a tall, tough-looking young fellow studying mechanical engineering, was a friend of the president of our chapel council. His way of dealing with the question at hand went something like this: "I know that I'm saved by grace alone, but my faith is a personal thing between God and me. If He calls me by His grace and I don't answer, nothing happens. What good is His calling if I don't respond?"

Tom was a "born again" Christian who had been converted in a small-group Bible study in his dormitory sponsored by one of the nondenominational "free lance" groups of Christians on campus. He had never really joined a church, feeling each one of them a bit too dogmatic for his blood. He just went from church to church as he felt like it, and he was at ours on this day.

"I wouldn't argue with you, Tom. Of course there needs to be a response. But there's more to it than you speak of. Let me ask you this: *How* did God call you? *Where* did He reach out to you? When you were all alone?"

"Of course not. I remember the day I made my decision for Christ. I'd been talking with a buddy for several months about religious questions. I could never quite get myself to make a commitment to Christ, though. I kind of wanted to, but I guess I was afraid. I didn't know what that might lead to. I remember being a little afraid of becoming a 'religious nut' of some kind. Then, too, I sort of felt that once I made a clear decision for Christ I would lose my freedom. I didn't know then that freedom comes *in* Christ, not by remaining free of Him.

"But then one day my buddy put it to me good. He accused me of putting off a decision I should have made a long time ago. He asked me if he could pray with me for courage to do what I knew I should do. I sort of hedged a bit and tried to put it off, but he insisted. I felt it wouldn't do any harm, so I said OK.

"Then it hit me like a ton of bricks. I *knew* that I had no choice anymore. God simply insisted that I join up with Him. So I did right then and there. It has changed my whole life."

I had to rejoice with him at this, but I pursued the question just a bit further: "You've sort of answered me, but I'd like to hear you say it plainly ... *how* did God call and *where* did He reach out to you?"

For a while Tom was puzzled. Finally he said, rather haltingly, "Well, I guess He spoke through my buddy. I don't know what else to say."

"That's exactly what I've been trying to get at," I said. "It was your friend who helped you 'find Jesus.' And the point of insisting on the importance of such an understanding is this—important though your personal decisions are, they are never *private* decisions. That's what the church is about: It's the public gathering of those who call themselves by the name of Christ. There, in public, they affirm together what it means to be Christian. There they support one another, encourage one another, join one another in prayer—all in the name of Christ, who has called them into His church. All of them have the same commitment you do, and they know that in sharing this commitment among themselves the commitment grows and is made stronger."

"That's all true, I guess. But what does that have to do with my insisting that I have to respond when God calls?"

"I was trying to point out that you would have nothing to respond to if it weren't for the church. In your case it happened to be your friend who kept carrying the message of the church, Christ crucified for your sins and raised again, to you. But *he* was the instrument by which God called. Your decision, personal though it was, became a possibility only as someone kept speaking to you and helped you grow into it.

"It may have seemed to happen all at once, in a sudden moment of clearly seeing something you'd thought about for quite some time. But it had a long history behind it. Your 'decision' had been in the making for months. Important though the moment you remember may have been, it was only one of many moments that went together to make up the calling of the Spirit to you."

Such discussions must seem like little more than playing with words to many people, but the point behind them is to express concern about undue emphasis on "decision making" in religion. If the decision—whether the *time* of decision or *manner* of decision making or the *experience* of the decision itself—becomes the all-important thing, it can easily lead to a number of deceptions. For example:

Undue emphasis on "decision making for Christ" may give the impression that it is really our humility or our submissiveness that opens the door for the Holy Spirit. The Spirit is the initiator of the call, however, and anything that suggests that we initiate the invitation to the Spirit to enter is a form of work-righteousness.

Undue emphasis on "decision making for Christ" very easily moves toward such a high "individualization" of the Christian faith as it is held by believers that it loses track of the importance of the church. When faith is so private that it does not relate to anyone else unless by accident, it is in danger of claiming its source within us rather than recognizing that faith is a public proclamation fostered in public and nourished in public. Moreover, it must be exercised in public. It is never just for private enjoyment.

Undue emphasis on "decision making for Christ" leads on occasion to an excessive appeal to the emotions. All too easily the decision becomes primarily an emotional response rather than a total response of body and mind along with the heart. If faith is understood to be basically an emotion, then either one is denying relatively unemotional people access to the faith or else one is making faith almost entirely a subjective response, since we are not always emotionally responsive. If it means that one believes only when one has achieved appropriate emotional levels, then faith is basically dependent on our whipping ourselves into proper emotional states. Although it is true that decisions can be and are made on levels other than emotions, "religion by decision" nearly always entails fairly heavy emotional involvement.

Undue emphasis on "decision making for Christ" leads rather commonly to inappropriate judgments over against people who have never had "experiences" or "decisions" of the sort required, but who have deep commitment to the same Christ claimed by those who practice "religion by decision." It is, perhaps, these judgments frequently made over against those who do not consciously remember any such time of unbelief, conversion, experience of Christ at a given time, etc., that is most revealing of the problems involved in practicing a "religion by decision." For it sounds, at least to those who are judged un-Christian or unfaithful, as though there is a self-righteousness about those who can "boast" of remembering times and places and particular occasions when faith came upon them.

Christians who have been baptized in infancy, raised in the

Word, and have grown through the Holy Supper can speak of "highs" and "lows" of faith, to be sure. They know that faith is not always as firmly seated within them as they should like. They can remember times when the Word of grace meant much more to them than usual—and also moments of doubt or anxiety when the Word of promise seemed almost impotent to move them. Therefore they can also remember flushes of faith—moments when, coming out of a low point, they were of a sudden caught up again into the glory of God's love and His marvelous grace swept over them again like a refreshing shower after a long drought.

This, however, is not a "decision for Christ," even though it is a tremendous moment of "experiencing God's love." It is not as though faith comes and goes and this surge of excitement upon feeling once again the full and free flow of God's love is the time when God first called us or when we first responded. It is part of the constantly growing experience of any Christian life with all its ebbs and flows. There are times of misery even in the faith, as well as times of glory. All of it together is the way the Spirit is working to bring our faith to its fullest fruition.

This requires constant interaction with other Christians around us, though. It is never purely a private enterprise, as I told Tom. That is why faith is always spoken of as both personal and public. What is personally held needs the constant discipline and correction of public exercise. Worship services, Bible studies, share groups, and other such Christian gatherings are ways in which this discipline and correction continues to take place. It is where children grow up into faith and adults mature in the faith. It is here where daily decisions are planted like seeds in the sharing of the community of faith. It is here where Christ's call is extended through the Word that is shared and where responses are made public.

"Religion by decision" does not intend to isolate Christians from such interactions and actively solicits their participation in such activities. We recognize that Bible studies and sharing groups are very important to those committed to this form of religious expression and are even seen in themselves as the source of a great deal of the evangelism emphasis so common to this way of living out the faith. That is what makes it hard to evaluate those times when people who cannot remember precise moments of decision or experience fall under their judgment and are called on to "receive Christ" so that they will be truly saved.

Erna was a very dedicated member of a neighboring parish whom I had known for a long time as a most knowledgable student of the Bible. She had begun attending a study and prayer group at the invitation of a neighbor and had thoroughly enjoyed it. She had told her pastor about it, so he knew that it had been very meaningful to her. That was why he was so surprised when she came in one day quite distraught.

The early part of the conversation went much like the one with which we opened this chapter. She had begun to question whether she was a Christian because she had not had an experience anything like all but one other person in the group had been able to remember. Her pastor asked her a simple question: "Do you believe that Jesus is God's Son and that He died for you and was raised again to give you hope?"

Her answer was an unequivocal and most fervent, "Yes!"

"Then why do you question whether you are a Christian?"

"Because I'm beginning to wonder if my answer to your question is only playing with words. The way my friends talk there is something very special about 'experiencing Christ,' and they talk about how it has changed their lives. I just don't know what it means to 'experience Christ,' but if I don't even know what it means, much less have it happen to me, then surely I have been kidding myself all these years and am not really a Christian at all." She was very upset, as her pastor could plainly see.

"Do you feel committed to Him right now? Are you willing to put your whole life on the line for Him, trusting Him even to death itself?"

"Yes, of course. But is that 'experiencing Christ'?"

"I'm sure there are many ways that might be used to describe this 'experience' of which you speak," her pastor told her. "But if you have the kind of commitment of which you speak—and I asked you that only because I wanted you to say what has been very plainly evidenced in your life as I have seen it—why worry about when or where or how that commitment became real within you? I doubt that you'll ever be able to track that down. You don't depend on your commitment so much as you depend on God's commitment to you, anyway, do you? After all, isn't it true that what counts is that *God* promised to take care of you? Now, mind you, that doesn't mean you can act irresponsibly over against God's promises. But it certainly means that when you ask if you are a Christian or not the key question isn't nearly so much how strongly you are committed to God as it is how strongly God is committed to you. And if you know that *His* commitment is so strong that nothing can break it (remember that passage in Romans about how nothing, neither

55

height nor depth, etc., can ever separate us from God's love?), then everything's OK! It's God's commitment to you that counts. Hang on to that, and everything else will fall into place."

Erna's pastor was giving her good advice. It was hard for her to drop the matter, though, and somehow it kept nagging at her for a long time. Since her husband had died some time before that and she wanted to pursue an education to equip her for a job in business, she entered the university some time after that. For a period of time she attended an independent church where this pressure for "decision" and "experience" continued to be applied. After long and agonizing weeks of continued study and sharing here in our community, a sort of "breakthrough" took place for her. She had felt for some time that she simply wasn't living up to Christian standards, and one day in a prayer session she suddenly "felt all her burdens lifted," to use her terminology, as she gave her life entirely to Christ's care and keeping. She had finally "experienced Christ," and she was radiant.

Now a new question was raised for her. She wanted to join that church where she had "found Christ," but discovered she could not without being baptized. Enough of her Lutheran upbringing hung on to her that she felt a bit ill at ease talking about being "baptized" when she had already been baptized long ago. Since that was not recognized as valid, however, she had to make a "decision" still again—this time about whether to submit to baptism a second time. She was mulling that question over when quite by accident she and I met at a function on campus.

In getting acquainted she discovered I was a Lutheran minister. She gave me the synopsis just narrated about her religious travels and asked me my advice. "Do you think I should get baptized again?"

I was a bit cautious lest I be misunderstood. "Do you believe that you were baptized once?"

"Of course I believe that. My parents told me about it and I have a baptismal certificate as a record of it."

"Then you can't really get 'baptized' again," I told her. "You may get immersed in water again in the name of the Trinity, but you'll only be going through some motions. For God doesn't play with these waters of our baptism. If you were baptized once, He was doing what He intended to do and told us He would do in the passages you're so familiar with in Holy Scripture."

She had never thought about it in just that way, but she reminded me that she could not join the church she now wished to join if she did not submit to rebaptism. "Is there any harm in it?" she asked.

I was even more cautious! One does not lightly play with another person's religious sensibilities. "I don't know that you can speak of 'harm' in being rebaptized, for the Bible never really even takes up the issue at all. It simply assumes there will only be one baptism. The question you are asking was never a question until people started insisting that one couldn't grow up into Christ but rather had to consciously decide for Him at a later date in life after one had come into what is usually called an 'age of responsibility,' 'age of accountability,' or some such name to indicate that decisions can now be personally made and accounted for by the individual him- or herself."

"What would you advise me to do?"

Such a forthright question called for a forthright and honest answer. I spoke as openly as I could. "I think it's playing games with baptism, if you want my honest opinion. I said a few moments ago that *God* doesn't play with the waters of our baptism and that He did in our baptism precisely what He promised to do. That's the faith of the church.

"If *we* now start playing with the waters of our baptism and suggest by a second baptism or in some other way imply that God was not or could not have been active in our baptism as infants because *we* were not at that time able to make our own personal decision about it, then we've called some basic elements of the idea of God's grace into question. Since you ask me, I must frankly say that I think any rebaptism is a serious questioning of the meaning and efficacy of baptism as such.

"Undoubtedly, then, the basic question you confront is this, 'What do you think baptism is?' And closely tied to it is the question of 'What constitutes a valid baptism?' When you've cleared those questions up for yourself, you'll have the answer to the question you asked me. For what it's worth, though, I hope you won't resent the straightforwardness and honesty with which I answer the question you ask me so openly."

That exchange around the question of rebaptism exposes, about as clearly as I know, the problems that lie in "religion by decision," for the insistence on making decisions for Christ is closely tied to the question of the nature of baptism. And when one speaks of baptism one is speaking of a primary channel God has given us for the offering of His grace to us in our need. If the efficacy of our baptism depends on our decision making, then surely it is plain that our decision making is the key to obtaining the grace of God. If our decision making is merely a response to God's grace, then our baptism is entirely independent of any decisions we make, but is purely and simply the announcement and sealing of God's good will to us as He names us by name and calls us into His family. That call, that decision on our behalf that ties itself closely to us by name in our baptism, is the beginning and origin of any and all decisions that follow on our part. That beginning of life in Christ, of course, needs nourishment and support, encouragement and admonition, discipline and shaping in its turn. That is what is offered by the Christian community within which God's grace continues to be available and offered through continued use of Word and sacrament. From beginning to end, the whole of our life in Christ is dependent on God's grace.

Does this wipe emotion out of faith? If we have seemed to assert that it does (and many people seem to assume that it indeed does), let us emphatically deny that here and now. To be sure, all too frequently worship services seem to be the epitome of sobriety and propriety, with hardly any hints of emotional involvement. With almost equal frequency the faith is discussed as though it had more to do with intellectual assent than it has to do with heartfelt commitment.

We raise the question especially so that we may vigorously say that we are not opposed to emotional involvement in religious commitment. Faith is filled with emotional content even though at the same time it must be measured in another sense by an intellectual content. That is quite different, however, from saying that faith is measured by how emotional a person is or that faith can be determined as present if the appropriate emotional response is made.

It is more like love, which has a deep emotional content while at the same time there are many other levels of involvement. Love cannot be measured by how emotionally a person expresses it, for mere infatuation is filled with gushing emotionalism. Love is expressed in word and deed at the same time that it carries deep emotional involvement and response.

So it is with faith. Although it may exhibit highly emotional qualities reaching deeply into the heart, it is ultimately and finally measured by the kinds of by-products it gives birth to. Does this faith show itself in patience, love, hope, and the many other gifts of the Spirit? The manifestation of faith itself, whether emotional or not, whether its origin in terms of time and place is known or not, has meaning only in the way it reveals itself to the world as the source of good works by which the name of God is glorified.

It will call forth many kinds of emotional response, then, as it filters through our person and works itself out into everyday living. It will enliven our singing and our praying in worship services, to be sure, even in liturgical services, which so many think must be dry and dusty. It will manifest itself in myriads of ways that will often appear emotional, particularly when it is at work in people who are naturally emotional to begin with.

None of this, however, makes faith itself just an emotion. We go to some pains to point this out because it is so often asserted that if religion does *not* call for decisions both public and private it must be devoid of emotion. That is simply not true, as is noted above. To say that faith has emotional consequences is quite a different thing from emphasizing an emotional experience or decision as being a determinative premise for the existence of true faith, though!

There are many sides to this question, as we have noted. It is by no means easy to maintain the necessary balance between God's grace and human response. Too strong an emphasis on God's grace easily leads to inactivity and a sort of fatalism that refuses to take any human responsibility in making necessary life decisions. Too strong an emphasis on human response, on the other hand, leads into the treacherous paths of self-justification and subtle forms of work-righteousness.

Steering a path between extremes is never easy. The fact that we feel the need to warn against a continually increasing emphasis on "religion by decision" dare never let us think that we have no need to stand accountable for our decisions and lives. Grace calls us to humility, not privilege! With proper humility, then, let us serve the Lord with gladness!

5

Religion by the Bible

If you did not pull up short at the title of this chapter, it failed in its purpose! It is meant to make the reader do a "double-take," for surely "religion by the Bible" would seem to be exactly what the Christian faith is all about. If we are not a religion of the Bible, then how would one describe us?

If you are given to watching for subtle changes, you perhaps noticed that the above paragraph pulled a "fast one" on you! The last sentence changed the title slightly from "religion *by* the Bible" to "a religion *of* the Bible." There may not be too much apparent difference at first glance, but upon closer inspection one detects a considerable difference indeed.

Randy had completed his doctorate a couple of years ago and had been teaching on the faculty here for a year and a half. He never missed church, and so when he was sick one Sunday morning it was natural for him to try to find a church service on the radio. He got more than he bargained for! He came to me the following Wednesday, just full of questions: "I heard this fellow on the radio talking about how the Bible tells us all kinds of things about the world today and how we're living in the end time. He said that we need to take note of how we should live and gave all kinds of rules he said we should follow about what to eat and stuff like that. He said he was getting it from the Bible, and he even gave chapters and verses of all kinds of books. But I couldn't tell what he was talking about. Where did he get all that stuff?

"I have to admit that he got it from the Bible," I said. "But I hardly consider it responsible use of the Bible. The Bible is like any book in the sense that you can pretty well do with it what you want, interpret it however you please, read into it whatever tickles your fancy. His use of the Bible leaves much to be desired!"

"But if he got it from the Bible, then it must be true," Randy said. "I always thought the Bible was true from cover to cover. How can he get it from the Bible and yet be wrong? I just thought that he was trying to fool me when he said he got it from the Bible. Now you tell me that everything he said was there! That bothers me more than when I thought he was making it up."

I explained to Randy that I did not mean to imply those *meanings* were in the Bible even though he was quoting *words* exactly from the Bible. In picking and choosing which words one will read—and sometimes equally important, which words one will *not* read!—one can suggest the Bible says all kinds of things that it never intends to say. "Let me give you an extreme example to show what I mean. The Scripture tells us that Judas went and hanged himself. It says elsewhere that we should go and do likewise. Is there any relationship whatever between those two passages?"

Randy was almost angry with me. "That's ridiculous!"

"Well, that's what I'm trying to say happens in so many 'interpretations' such as you heard on the radio. If you listen carefully to where these people quote their Scripture references from, you'll find they draw the so-called proofs of what they're saying from widely separated and altogether unrelated places in the Bible. When they string them together in whichever fashion they choose, though, they come out sounding rather acceptable and sometimes downright compelling to people with a strong commitment to the Bible. It caught *your* attention, didn't it? People who have a 'religion by the Bible' find it a powerful attraction."

Randy asked if Christians do not have a "religion by the Bible," and that got us back to where we started this chapter.

Perhaps the key question for our concern at this point could be asked in this way: Just what *is* the Bible?

Some people understand the Bible to be basically a code book which, if properly deciphered, gives one access to the very mind of God.

Some people understand the Bible to be basically a sort of catechism with answers for any and every question that may come to our attention.

Some people understand the Bible to be basically a presentation of certain beliefs and doctrines that are to be dug out of various parts of the Bible without regard to the setting in which they appear, are to be pieced together into a whole, and then must be believed in just that way.

Interestingly enough, the question of what the Bible *is* was not very much disputed among Christian people until only two and a half centuries or so ago. There was general unanimity among Christians as to what the Bible *is,* and the major questions asked revolved more around how to interpret some of the passages of the Bible.

The subject of this chapter, "religion by the Bible," has taken a new twist within the last couple centuries and imposes itself on us in a special way in our own day. We need to consider the two questions of what the Bible is and how to interpret it rather independently at this point in order to make proper distinctions in our concerns, even though they are interrelated.

We first examine some of the assertions suggested about what the Bible *is,* for there are many who would hold one or several of the understandings proposed above as the best way to speak of the basic intent of the Bible. None of those proposals, however, have been considered good definitions of the Biblical intent until in the relatively recent past! We will have to contrast those understandings, therefore, with the more generally accepted understandings of Christian faith as we go along.

Jesse was a member of a ministerial association in a town where I once served as pastor. I had a number of long and most interesting conversations with him about these very things. He was a firm believer in looking at every minute detail of the Bible to determine how God thought. He was a "decoder" of the first rank! He was sure that he knew the very mind of God, for he could quote the most obscure passages imaginable and put them together with other passages. It made one stand in awe to see how he could put such passages together in order to determine the intimate truths of the divine mind. I have never known anybody so filled with Biblical verses pumped out almost at will in any order that fit his needs so far as I could see.

He had taken virtually every name in the Bible and made it fit some contemporary nation or person. He had found passages I would never have dreamt of and had fitted them into a pattern clearly setting forth the unfolding history of the world, showing how God had thought everything out in minutest detail. He never doubted for a moment that he had discovered the whole of God's intentions and ways with humanity. It was as though the Bible were an open door into the very mind of God. At least Jesse was sure that was what it was!

The question is raised, though, as to whether the Bible is best described as revealing God's mind—or His heart! If it reveals His mind and our primary purpose in studying the Bible is to decipher the code with which He has revealed His mind, then we are really saved by "knowing" what we have decoded rather than by believing in Christ. Faith is thereby reduced basically to believing that what God's mind thinks is revealed in the Bible. This approach to the Bible seriously undermines its whole intention.

It is not an uncommon approach to the Bible today, though. Many people are quite caught up in intricate efforts to decipher the real meaning of this code book from God. Such people would say the Bible is a revelation of God's mind.

The second suggestion is rather different in the way it is approached, but it remains essentially the same in terms of its final outcome.

Joan, mother of three very active children and wife of one of the more prominent men in town, belonged to a church that had taken strong positions on a wide variety of theological beliefs and social issues. We served on a citizen's committee together, assessing certain mental health needs of the community. I got to know her quite well over the course of time.

I was amazed at how readily she had answers to the most complex questions (evidently reflecting her church's answers) simply by quoting the Bible. The committee on which we were serving had to do with drug usage at our local school, so it encompassed a wide variety of subjects that came under discussion—family life, personal identity, anxieties raised by our age, school and community administrative decisions, and so on. For every issue that arose Joan had an immediate answer from the Bible. She never seemed to give leeway for discussion, nor were there any alternatives to the answers she gave so far as she was concerned, for what the Bible said was true and that ended the discussion.

She was not a "decoder" like Jesse was. For her the Bible was a series of answers to any question life or religion might raise, though. Again, she had at her disposal a vast storehouse of memory verses. They were very different kinds of passages from those used by Jesse, though, and these were usually much better-known passages than Jesse was inclined to use.

There was the time, for example, when we were talking about family relationships and the increasingly diminishing control parents exercised over their children. We were questioning what forces were at work to either cause the children to disregard their parents' wishes so openly or why parents would permit this to happen. "It is because nobody takes the Bible seriously any more," Joan said. "It is plainly stated, 'Thou shalt honor thy father and thy mother,' and nobody even cares that God says that."

We all agreed that was the ideal and obedience was to be desired, but we pointed out the complexities introduced into that simple word by modern society. Applying the commandment is a bit more complicated than just quoting it to parents or children. Another member of the committee, in fact, who was also deeply committed to the Christian faith and often spoke of it as openly as Joan did, was having great difficulty with one of his children just at this time. He certainly knew and believed and tried to apply the commandment, but it all seemed counterproductive and he was rather offended at Joan's suggestion that just pushing hard on that commandment would straighten everything out. He took that word seriously, but not much was straightening out for him. Joan would not budge, though. That was the needed word.

I had coffee wth her on occasion and since she knew I was a minister she talked more openly with me in these less formal settings. She seemed appalled that I did not take the Bible more seriously as an "answer book" for every question. I tried to assure her that I believed the Bible contains the very basic answers to the fundamental needs of our life, but I could never convince her that one could not draw specific passages into the picture to deal with every contemporary issue, whether it be the appropriateness of the use of nuclear energy for generating power or the question of whether one should place an aged grandmother into a nursing home or not. For her all questions could be answered from the Bible if only one looked in the proper place.

This was even more especially true when it came to religious questions. One always had to stand in awe at the certainty and quickness with which she would respond to "faith" questions. Often she would not even quote the passage entirely. "How is one saved?" "John 3:16 tells you!" "Is divorce ever permissible?" "Whoever divorces his wife and marries another, commits adultery against her; and if she divorces her husband and marries another, she commits adultery. Mark 10:11-12." "What is a woman's place in church?" "1 Timothy 2:11 says: 'Let a woman learn in silence with all submissiveness.'" "What is the meaning of baptism?" "Read Romans 6:1-11." Rarely did I ever hear her hesitate. She knew exactly what the answer to every religious question was and where it was to be found in the Bible.

Although she functioned on an altogether different level from that on which Jesse functioned, the end result was much the same. Anyone who knew Joan was aware that one could expect an answer from the Bible for any question they asked—which is substantially

64

the same again as saying that she had an inside track on what God thought about everything. All one has to do is to know the mind of God well enough and one can deal with any situation of life.

Again we encounter a salvation by "knowing" the mind of God and living by it—which begins to move toward salvation by a proper life lived in accord with knowing what God wants of us. God's heart is not seriously a part of the picture in such an approach, though. Only His will is reckoned with as it is directed by the revelation of what He thinks to be good or not.

This understanding of the Bible needs to caution us about how to use catechisms as instructional tools. It is all too easy to translate the use of Bible passages under appropriate questions and answers into an implication that the whole Bible is an answer book. This is hardly to say that there is anything wrong using "proof passages" wisely chosen and proper to the material. Nor does it imply anything wrong with catechetical instruction as such. It is rather to warn against implying through such use that the Bible is basically an "answer book" or that "proof passages" are points of entry into the mind of God, giving us special information that is the essential stuff of salvation.

Such an implication would be a return to a very old heresy dating back to New Testament times, when some people were trying to import certain pagan ideas, teaching that salvation hinged on "knowing divine mysteries" or "having access to the secrets of God." The Book of Colossians addresses such problems in particular, although warnings against it are sprinkled throughout the New Testament.

The position just described is very similar to the third suggestion we noted earlier, in which the Bible is viewed as a source book for beliefs and doctrines that are dug out of various parts of the Bible without regard to the setting in which they appear, are pieced together again into a whole, and then must be believed in just that way. Yet there are again certain points of distinction between the two, similar though they may be on the surface.

Quite some time ago an article appeared in a paper of Christian origin telling of a discovery by astronomers that a humming or singing sound emanated from many stars due to light rays, X rays, and other such radiations from their surface. In electronically operated telescopes that scan stars in ways other than mere optical examination (some of them actually being radio scans) these sounds could be picked up, whereas previous telescopes that could only take visual sightings of the stars had never been able to detect this. The article triumphantly pointed to passages such as "The morning stars sang together" (Job 28:7) and "Sing, O heavens, for the Lord has done it" (Is. 44:23) to show that God had not deceived us in inspiring His Word for our instruction! Indeed the Bible had again been proved in its detail with this astronomical demonstration.

Such examples can be multiplied by reading in certain types of religious literature or listening to some of the already mentioned radio programs or moving in certain circles of the church. The Bible is cited over and over again to show how "accurately" it depicts certain knowable phenomena (carefully avoiding references that are beyond such evidence or proof so far as we can determine), extrapolating from that kind of evidence the trustworthiness of Scripture also and especially in realms that lie beyond demonstration. Thus we are confronted with undeniable proofs in the visible world that Scripture can be trusted in its every detail.

That becomes the stepping-stone, then, to propose almost anything and everything that may come to mind. If the Bible has been proved on "knowable" grounds, surely one can and *must* trust it on grounds beyond our knowing and proving. The ways Bible passages can then be strung together to make up networks of faith boggle the mind!

The millennial groups of which we spoke at considerable length in the third chapter, for example, draw on 10 verses of one chapter of the Bible to establish the foundation for their entire description of the end times. As we suggested, there are many, many variations of the millennial schemes, but none of them could exist at all without the 10 verses that open the 20th chapter of John's Revelation. The Bible has no reference to these thousand years at any other place than this. Since, however, the Bible is "proved" as trustworthy in all its parts, a literal understanding of these thousand years is necessary. Once this frame of reference is established as the basic point of departure for understanding the last days of the earth, passages (in isolation from their context to a very large extent) from all over the Scriptures are considered eligible for introduction into this same picture.

Our concern here, though, is not simply that a mere 10 verses constitute the foundation for a whole network of faith. It has to do with the nature of the Bible. Is it a giant container of facts and philosophy with all its parts scattered around waiting for us to put them together in proper order? In that case the task of one faithful to its intent could well be to study all its parts in detail, take it apart, and then rearrange it in accordance with what are perceived to be

God's (but are likely to be one's own) religious, philosophical, and even political principles.

If Joan's view was that the Bible could answer any question and thus became a sort of ethical and religious guidebook, the view we have just been describing makes of it a religious/philosophical book with the giant scheme of God's salvation hidden within it waiting for pious people to find. The "provable" parts related to visible reality are basically to establish its reliability on the levels that really count! This is a form of Jesse's decoding, but it leads into a more philosophical world than Jesse ever worked with, for he stayed pretty well on the level of understanding the world in which we presently must live.

We do not mean to scorn the use of the Bible to establish doctrine, of course. That is quite different from what we have been describing, though.

Use of the Bible to establish the Christian faith system is concerned with viewing the whole sweep of Biblical truth and organizing that sweep of teaching into something of an ordered outline. What we have been describing above is just the opposite, for it looks at all the detail and tries to order it into a broad sweep of teaching without much regard for the plain thrusts that run throughout the whole of Scripture. It frequently even disregards the immediate context from which the detail is lifted, for that matter.

Once again, of course, we are encountering the "knowledge" factor, although now it is more a philosophical knowledge gaining certain provable footholds by means of demonstrable evidences in the material world. Faith remains, however, "believing" that what is revealed in this rearrangement of details is "true beyond a shadow of a doubt." The Christian faith is imperceptibly turned from believing in Christ to believing that the Bible is true, a subtle shift from faith to knowledge.

When I was trying to explain something of this to a Bible class some time ago the question was raised, "But isn't it true that the Bible is the Word of God? If that's true, then isn't it correct to say that whether we believe the Bible or not is a test of whether we believe God or not?" As you can perhaps imagine, that launched us into quite a discussion.

I won't try to repeat all of that discussion here, but permit just a brief recounting of the main thrust of what came out of that discussion.

To be sure, in Christian circles, the Bible is commonly called the Word of God. It is *not,* however, considered primarily a book that gives us access to God's mind, but to His heart! It indeed has information in it, but it is basically the story of how God has dealt with and promises to continue to deal with the human race. It is, therefore, basically a book telling of how God has acted in, reacted to, and interacts with human history.

The basic problem of the positions discussed in the last several pages is that they remove the Bible from the world of history to which it is addressing itself and make it speak instead primarily to a world of thought, of philosophy, of expositions of the mysteries of heaven. For all that one could say about the Bible being a "window to heaven," it is a very small window when compared to the treasures of what God's mind holds. But it is above all a window to His heart, a way of understanding how He deals with humans who have left their Father in search of their own future. Faith is not a flight into the secrets of heaven, but a very real encounter with God right in the midst of the concrete everydayness of human living.

While the Bible certainly has thoughts and theological/ philosophical meditations within it, and while it reveals divine mysteries through the small window mentioned, this inspired book tells how God could never turn His people loose even when they rebelled against His rule, struggled against His mercy, and sought their own way. From the very opening of the Bible, where His creative hand is revealed as being fatherly and loving, to the very end of the Bible, where His Son's victory through the cross over the forces of evil is offered as the ultimate hope of humanity, the Bible reveals a divine heart that cannot stand idly by while His people are held captive in sin. That is its whole thrust as it speaks of His forming a special people for Himself in Israel and again in the church in order to give continuing testimony to this love of God that pursues us even in the midst of our rebellion.

The Bible, then, is primarily a revelation of God's love (and His judgment) expressed in the meaning and direction of history. It is far more than merely a philosophical revelation of divine mysteries. It is in fact the broad sweep of divine love exposing a Father's heart that cries out to His sinful children to return home, to entrust themselves to the arms that can and will protect them against the threats that surround the human course of life every step of its way. It is a Word that invites us in turn to enter this thrust of history initiated by His grace and to become involved as His children in making a new thing of the history in which we participate.

To understand this, one must work with the large sweeps of history that move through the Old and New Testaments. The details show how this all worked out, particularly as God dealt with the history of His chosen people Israel. But the details are not to be lifted out of their context and dealt with as independent truths to be strung together in whatever way a person chooses to combine them in order to uncover some deep and hidden mystery of heavenly dimensions.

That is the basic difference between seeing the Bible as a revelation of God's head or a revelation of His heart. Entire books are written on this, so what we say here in no way pretends to be an exhaustive analysis. Yet we hope the difference is plain enough to distinguish between "religion *by* the Bible" and a "religion *of* the Bible." A "religion *of* the Bible" will recognize the deep mysteries that will always lie beyond human understanding. It searches for the revelation of how God deals with His people even and especially when we do not have the foggiest understanding of what is happening around us. "Religion *by* the Bible" has as a primary item on its agenda the uncovering of such mysteries and the revelation of such things as only God could know. Thus it longs for and looks for revelations by which it can gain access to salvation through *knowledge* of the divine so that it can indeed understand *everything* that is happening around and within us.

That becomes rather subtle on occasion, but it is a most important distinction to make. As we suggested earlier, it is something very old in the world of Christendom since it was one of the first heresies that had to be repudiated, the heresy called "gnosticism" (meaning "knowledge" and referring to those who asserted one would be saved at least in part by acquiring knowledge of divine mysteries). At the same time, the form in which it appears today is very new, for to a considerable extent it seems to be a reaction and response to the world of "knowledge" that science has fostered.

Ever since the early 19th century, believers have tried to defend the Bible against certain assaults on it by science. Nearly all such efforts have strongly emphasized the total reliability and trustworthiness of Scripture.

Now, while we certainly agree that the Bible is inspired by God and is reliable and trustworthy in all its parts, we must still question the basic premises we have spoken about earlier regarding the *nature* of the Bible. What *is* the Bible? It is not a book gaining entry to God's head, but a book revealing God's heart. There is the heart of any controversy we might have with "religion by the Bible."

The second part of the controversy has now begun to enter the picture rather prominently. We have started talking more and more about ways to *interpret* the Bible. How one views the nature of the

Bible, of course, will determine much of how one proceeds to interpret the book. But we hope it will be profitable to look a little more closely at this second question, interpretation.

Perhaps a little story will help illustrate the point. Bob, a young accountant in town, was talking with me one day as we sat by the swimming pool. Jane, whom I knew only casually, came up and sat down beside us. I quickly gathered she was a secretary working in the same office complex where Bob had his office.

Things seemed pleasant enough, and then my attention was diverted by one of my children asking me to do something. When I returned to the conversation, things had heated up considerably. Somehow their discussion had turned to some event scheduled on the Saturday following, and Bob's church insisted that one must worship on Saturday. Apparently he had said something about profaning the Sabbath Day and inappropriate activities on Saturday, for they had become embroiled in quite a controversy. "It is plain in the Bible," Bob said, "that the Sabbath is Saturday. Why don't you take the Bible seriously?"

Jane took considerable offense at this, for she, too, was a devout member of her church, although it taught nothing about observing Saturday as the day of worship. She insisted that the Old Testament had basically been replaced by the New Testament, which said nothing about what day to worship on. She quoted the passage in Colossians about no one judging you in regard to the Sabbath (Col. 2:16).

This exchange exemplifies one of the problems that arise even and sometimes especially among people committed strongly to the basic authority of the Bible itself. One can find any number of Bible passages that seem to support given positions so that even among people mutually committed to the *authority* of the Bible there still arise multitudes of questions about who is right and who is wrong. Do you decide that on the basis of who can find the *most* Bible passages? Or on the basis of who can find the seemingly *clearest* Bible passages? Or on the basis of who can count the most people on their side in interpreting passages? Or on the basis of who can argue his/her case most convincingly? None of these are good answers to begin with, and certainly none of them clear the air even if they are applied.

How, then, does one deal with this problem?

Perhaps the first thing that needs to be done is to recognize something of what is indeed a proper intuition on the part of those who follow "religion *by* the Bible" even though it gets turned into

70

some odd and misplaced channels in its concern to "defend the Bible." That intuition is to take the Bible as literally as possible. We need to hear that loudly and clearly, for the Bible is not to be played with nor made light of. When it speaks, the Christian person is concerned about listening. It is our instructor; it is not for us to instruct the Scriptures! We need to keep that straight.

That means, then, that wherever and whenever possible we need to understand the Bible literally. There is really nothing new about that, for it has been the view of the church through the ages.

The question of interpretation does not revolve around the word "literal," which nearly all Christians agree with in one way or another, but rather around the phrase "wherever and whenever possible."

Even the most extreme literalist understands that when Scripture says, "I say to God, my rock . . ." (Ps. 42:9) it does not mean that God is a rock. That is a figure of speech. Literal interpretation needs to take into account at the very least the rules of language, understanding poetry to be something quite different from prose, parables to be different from history, and so on.

That, of course, is only the surface of the problem, for the more intensely one pursues the "wherever and whenever possible" phrase, the more deeply one gets caught in a web of interpretational difficulties. Luther and Zwingli parted ways over the simple little word "is" as it was used by Christ in instituting the Lord's Supper. Luther insisted that "is" meant just what it says, while Zwingli insisted that it contradicts reason to accept "is" at face value since there is no way of understanding how Jesus can indeed be present at every place and every time bread and wine are offered with the words, "This is My body . . . this is My blood." He wanted to make it mean "represents." Luther wanted nothing to do with that, since it was tampering with Scripture to make words mean something other than what they plainly say. The one simple word became a major barrier between their understandings and their fellowship.

Problems of interpretation are not easily solved. To hear millennialists talk, one would assume that the thousand years' reign of Christ is one of the clearest things taught in Holy Scripture, if one takes the 20th chapter of John's Revelation literally. But, there is so much disagreement among millennialists about the details of this millennium that it quickly becomes apparent that it is not really all that plain. This happens, of course, because when one picks out such a relatively isolated section as the key to the whole of Scripture, then how the whole picture will look when you are finished depends on how you take the rest of the Bible apart and fit it back together again within this supposed millennial chain of events. Everything depends on where you insert what passage, and the whole becomes a potpourri of pious ideas that have no real grounding in sound Biblical interpretation. It's largely a case of those who hold these private ideas seeking Biblical reference by lifting any passage convenient for supporting the "truth" they are trying to prove or for filling in the "scheme" they are convinced John was trying to set forth.

The danger and problem with this is that in the end one can become so preoccupied with trying to fit all the pieces into their proper places that one loses the basic thrust of the whole Scripture—the saving grace of God. Instead of keeping eyes on that, one instead becomes so absorbed in solving the "puzzle of the Scriptures" that the truth of Scripture is lost in the detail with which one is working so tediously.

If, then, the method of being literal wherever and whenever possible does not resolve the question as thoroughly as we might hope, are we simply at an end of our possibilities?

"Religion *by* the Bible" tends to affirm this as the sole criterion, resorting to some of the suggestions mentioned earlier (counting passages, gathering as much support as possible, etc.) when no agreement can be reached on literal meanings. "Religion *of* the Bible," however, points to a variety of other available aids. None of them are perfect, nor do any of them resolve all the difficulties. That is quite obvious, for denominations have existed long before the current style of "religion *by* the Bible" arose in Christendom. Differences of interpretational opinion have existed from the very beginning of the Christian era . . . and there were differences of interpretational opinion among the Jews regarding the Old Testament before Christ appeared on the scene. So we offer nothing to entirely resolve this very old dilemma other than some checks and balances that have been built into the way the church deals with such interpretational questions. They should be mentioned here as a way of showing how "religion *by* the Bible" shortchanges the sound resources available to serious students of the Scriptures.

We shall speak of them briefly under three headings:

(1) All interpretation of Scripture must be generated out of the plainly stated major thrusts of the Bible. The commonly accepted phrase to describe this is: "Scripture must always interpret Scripture."

(2) Scripture belongs to the entire church. It is therefore not merely a private book nor subject to purely private interpretations.

(3) The tradition of the church must be kept in mind when interpreting Scripture, for throughout history there has been a sifting of understandings that have helped clarify what may be considered proper and what must be considered wrong in the teachings of the church.

The first of these three headings ("Scripture interprets Scripture") helps interpreters avoid isolating an idea found only in one small part of the Bible and using it as the key to understanding all other sections of the Bible. Interpretation must work the other way around—the major thrusts of the Bible must be considered basic and developed thoroughly as the foundation for anything and everything that is taught as Christian faith. All smaller sections or less clear sections, no matter how intriguing they appear to be or how much they may catch our fancy as interesting thoughts to be developed, must always be subject to interpretation through the plainer and most commonly taught thrusts of the Bible.

Luther experienced the judgment of God under the Law as the force that opened to him the full glory of the Gospel message of God's grace and forgiveness. This became the key to understanding Scripture for all Lutheran comprehensions of the Christian faith— the polarity of Law and Gospel. This pervasive thrust of the Bible, found from Genesis to Revelation, provides the basic background for any interpretational questions that people in the Lutheran tradition may wrestle with.

John Calvin perceived the sovereignty of God's rule as the point of departure for all interpretational activity. Others have spoken of the warming and enlightening work of the Spirit, under whom Scripture was inspired, as being the primary thrust of all Scriptural interpretation. And there are still others.

It is *this* kind of disagreement that has stood behind the basic divisions of the church. One must be careful lest one is deceived by this, however, for there are only five or six such major points of departure for the interpretational activity of the church . . . not hundreds as may appear from the denominational scheme with which we live in America. To be sure, these major points of departure have in their turn divisions of their own. But these are more like "family disagreements" and are by no means the same as the major theological points of departure for interpretational problems with which we are here concerned.

Each of this rather limited number of basic points of departure obviously has a strong enough basis to sustain its position, for they have all survived the larger test of time. Perhaps the real task of ecumenical efforts is the integration of these several bases into a unified whole so that the integrity of each of these major thrusts is preserved while enriching the others in turn without destroying them.

At any rate, when one is undertaking the detailed task of interpreting Scripture one must be keenly aware of these possible approaches. Nearly always a strong commitment to one of them will be consciously kept in mind, for that matter, since nearly every interpreter has been touched by these possibilities in a major way through denominational affiliation. There is nothing wrong with this and it can even be helpful so long as the person is aware of his/her own "bias," for it can help "measure" what one is doing. That is quite different, though, from each person just doing one's own thing, thus making the Bible a field for any kind of private interpretation one chooses to impose on it.

This also distinguishes the Christian interpretation of the Bible from other religions, such as Judaism and Islam, that refer to the whole or parts of the Bible as authority for their understandings. The Christian perceives the Bible as a whole, a unit, one complete account of God's gracious activity among mankind. The Old Testament is always looking toward the New Testament, anticipating some fulfillment bigger than it can see on its own. The New Testament is written with the Old Testament very much in mind, understanding the person and work of Jesus through the perspectives that the Old Testament lend to Him. Neither testament alone can give us the whole of faith. Each has its own integrity, but neither is entirely understandable apart from the other. The whole of Scripture is necessary for the interpretation of any of Scripture!

The discussion by the swimming pool mentioned a little while ago is illustrative of this point. Jane was quite right in quoting the New Testament when Bob insisted on an observance of the Sabbath based on the Old Testament alone. Truth lies in the joining of the intent of the Sabbath observed in the Old Testament with the Christ who fulfilled all Old Testament intentions.

The same principal covers many attempts at extending Old Testament laws into New Testament practice. For instance, dietary laws (which some people stretch to cover even blood transfusions) and other such rituals and laws prescribed in the Old Testament all find their ultimate meaning and fulfillment in the coming of Christ. This is a fundamental Christian understanding.

One must be cautious, therefore, about isolating promises as well as laws made to a particular people at a particular time from the larger intention that those promises carried. For instance, no matter how much one may admire the Jewish people and sympathize with them in the many unjust sufferings they have endured, any attempt to take the Old Testament promises giving the Holy Land to God's ancient people and making those same promises applicable to the reestablishment of the nation of Israel today is highly problematic, to say the least. Israel's present nationhood is born of contemporary political decision-making, and authentication with Biblical promises of old presents many difficulties. In utilizing Scripture to interpret Scripture one must not take specifics and broaden them to generalities, as in turn one cannot take generalities and turn them into specifics.

In these and many other ways the principle that "Scripture must always interpret Scripture" keeps a balance in interpretations and helps maintain the integrity even while it stresses the interdependence of the Old and New Testament.

We spoke above about the dangers of an extreme kind of private interpretation of Scripture. That leads to the second of the major headings mentioned earlier, namely, that Scripture belongs to the entire church.

It comes as something of a surprise to many people when they are told that the Biblical writers probably never expected their material to be read privately by individuals. That fact is obvious, though, once one thinks about it. At least two things tell us this rather plainly:

On the one hand all literature in the days when the books of the Bible were coming into being was hand copied. There were no printing presses or mimeographs to mass produce written material. Therefore only very wealthy people or "libraries" of some kind could ever have written material at their disposal. At least in part that is why monasteries, where much of the copying was done, were the repositories of much of the written materials in Christian history. They contained the "libraries."

On the other hand, not many people were able to read in those times. Most common people used memory for storage of materials that were to be passed on, much more than written documents. Only the wealthy or a very select group of people ever had need to learn how to read, for that matter, since only they had access to written material, on the average. Probably the Jews in general had more literacy than most people of their time, but even among them there was little written material available to the average person for private use.

What does this have to do with the suggestion that Scripture is the property of the entire church? It simply means that virtually all use of Scripture from earliest times was in the *public* proclamation of the Word. Private devotional reading would be all but unknown save in monasteries or in certain select places. The Bible was never considered a "private" book or even a "personal" book. It was the "book of the church." All interpretation was virtually forced into public forums. Even those public forums were not, like so many of ours today, radio or TV programs going into the homes of people although originating in the privacy of broadcasting booths. Any time it was heard, it had to be heard personally from a reader to a listener and discussed publicly! It could not be one person's private opinion foisted on a whole lot of people. Even when Bible interpretation more and more fell to the decisions of a church hierarchy, it still had public forums by virtue of Scripture being read in the services and shared, as it were, with the people. The hierarchy in its turn shared and discussed the Scriptures within forums of their own. If what seemed an improper or disrespectful opinion of passages or sections of Scripture was voiced, a public forum called it to task.

Scripture was, therefore, not written or meant to be a "private book," but it was and is still the "book of the church." Its interpretation must always take place on levels where the interaction of Christian people gives balance and the opportunity to correct drastically erring ways.

This leads us to the third "check and balance" that the church has always worked with when it was at its best in interpretational methodology—a deep awareness of "the tradition of the church." This is not to say that tradition is infallible or unerring, but it is to say that anyone who disregards the history of the church's interpretational efforts runs the risk of making some of the same basic errors that were refuted by the church long ago. An old error tried today does not make any better interpretational material now than it did then!

Very early the church had to start a sort of "sifting process" of interpretations, for very many opinions (many of them indeed private and ill-founded) had started circulating within it. For us who inherit the faith in the forms we know today it may appear that the church has always had such understandings. Upon examining this early history of the church, however, one discovers great struggles to determine just what should and what should not be given place in the church's understanding of Christian faith. Even rather simple "truths" we receive today had to be refined in the struggle of the church through the ages.

That does not mean that doctrine is simply tradition, for this struggle took place around the very subject we have been considering in this chapter—how does one interpret the Scripture? Many varying opinions had to be taken into account and sifted through the public understandings of Christian people, then refined in formal councils of the church and tried once more in the public forum of Christian worship and life. Many so-called "heresies" as we identify them today had a life of longer or shorter duration in the early history of the church and proved incapable of standing up to Scriptural evidence and Christian faith and life. That was not always seen immediately, but had to be discovered only as the "heresy" (as we know it) had been given reasonable hearing in the life of the church.

That is why the tradition of the church is so important to the continuing interpretation of the Scriptures. If some of these old teachings reappear (and on occasion the old heresies appear in such new dress that at first they are hard to spot . . . many cults of today are good examples of this) we need to be able to repudiate them without having to go through all that the early church went through. There is no need to repeat the old heresies over and over again, for they have been given hearings (some of them have received several hearings) and been repudiated time after time.

This means again, though, that interpretation is not a private matter. If contemporary interpretation is to be done within the check and balance of all believers together sharing and being involved in the understanding of Scripture, it is also true that contemporary interpretation needs to be very much aware of how understandings and interpretations have been passed through the ages.

It may sound as though this limits interpretation to scholars of history, but that is not so. We need to listen to historians and be open to the insights they can give us about what is and has been acceptable and what has been repudiated and therefore should be repudiated again today. But there are simple statements of this that have been built through the ages as the way by which Christians tie themselves historically to this unfolding understanding of what is basic and irrefutable in the confession and life of the church. We call them the "ecumenical creeds." Two of the three are used very extensively in the worship life of the church, the Apostles' Creed and the Nicene Creed. In these simple ways the ages have given to us in short form some basic guidelines for what must be confessed to be at the very heart of the Christian heritage.

These checks and balances, as we have called them, are important parts of the task of interpretation. They give room for the scholars who make detailed analyses, but they draw all Christians together into the common task of interpreting the Scriptures. One person can never do it for all people.

Thus the place of the Bible is very strongly maintained in "religion of the Bible" while it warns against some of the privatistic or "history-less" excesses of "religion by the Bible." By God's grace we will never lose Scripture as our basis for Christian faith and life, the norm for all that is taught and done in the church. But it must be kept and maintained within the constraints of the checks and balances noted here—or else the Bible becomes the ground for anybody to do with as one pleases, "prove" whatever idea strikes one's fancy with whatever Bible passages meet the needs of the moment, and attempt to pass such assertions on to the church as the very Word of God.

The constantly increasing access to all forms of public media on the part of religious practices of every stripe has given a grand opportunity for those who wish to bombard Christians with some extremely strange notions in the name of the Bible. This chapter is designed to warn against such "religion by the Bible" and to encourage again the very best devotion to that faith and practice given us by the Spirit in the words of that book which points us always and only to *the* Word made flesh, Jesus Christ our Lord.

6

Religion by Authority

You see them everywhere—on street corners, in airports, on parking lots. Sometimes they solicit money directly, pleading causes such as drug programs. At other times they are selling flowers or candy, telling you the proceeds are going to some socially beneficial project.

They work long hours without pay. They are indefatiguable in promoting their cause openly or in more hidden ways as noted above. They are intensely dedicated people.

They are cult members.

The increasing popularity of all kinds of cults, especially among the young of our day, is one of the most apparent—and strange— phenomena of our time.

A "cult" by definition is a strongly authoritarian religious group that exists, sometimes very intentionally and at other times quite unintentionally, *outside* the basic Christian frame of reference. Under the influence of a strong leader, a cult carries the "religion by the Bible" ideas we discussed in the previous chapter much further—so far, in fact, that the group can no longer be legitimately called Christian. As we have noted in the case of other aberrations, many cult manifestations are old heresies presented in new dress.

Walter Martin, in his book *The Kingdom of the Cults,* quotes a definition of Dr. Charles Braden as follows: "By the term 'cult' I mean nothing derogatory to any group so classified. A cult, as I define it, is any religious group which differs significantly, in some one or more respects as to belief or practice, from those religious groups which are regarded as the normative expressions of religion in our total culture." Mr. Martin, in turn, adds, "... a cult might also be defined as a group of people gathered about a specific person or person's interpretation of the Bible." (From p. 11 of the cited work by Mr. Martin. Minneapolis: Bethany Fellowship, Inc. Martin quotes Dr. Braden from a work entitled *These Also Believe,* Preface, xii.)

With greater harshness Dave Breese says in *Know the Marks of Cults:* "A cult is a religious perversion. It is a belief and practice in the world of religion which calls for devotion to a religious view or leader centered in false doctrine. It is an organized heresy." (Wheaton, Ill.: Victor, 1976.)

If one examines all these definitions and others that could be quoted alongside them, one finds a thread running through them that we have chosen to identify in this chapter as "religion by authority." In every case a "cult" is identified with a strong authority. Usually this is a person, although it may be on occasion an authoritative writing or teaching. This strong authority establishes everything to be taught, how adherents shall live, and all that is necessary for the perpetuation of the movement.

For our purposes here, then, we shall speak of a "cult" as a religious group that has deviated so significantly from the religious thought that gave it birth as to have manifestly formed a *new* and *altered* stream of faith and life.

Dr. Martin says in his *The Kingdom of the Cults:* "From a theological viewpoint, the cults contain not a few major deviations from historic Christianity. Yet paradoxically, they continue to insist that they are entitled to be classified as Christians" (p. 11).

To be even more specific, although Martin ties cults to *Christian* thought in the previous quotation, a cult may well be a deviation from the basic norm of *any* major world religious belief. Many contemporary cults are offshoots of Eastern religious beliefs, while a few others are offshoots of Islamic or Judaic faith systems. Every religion seems to be subject to the development of cults springing out of it.

All legitimate forms of the Christian religion have a strong sense of authority. That is why we are so concerned about proper distinctions here. The authority to which Christianity always points is the book of Holy Scriptures. In Christian circles the faith confessed must always originate in the Bible.

"Religion by authority," however, looks far more to the interpreter than the book, whether the book be the Bible, the Koran, or some other religious holy book. The book cannot be understood properly at all without the presence of or interpretive word from those who are authoritative spokespeople for cultic forms of the religions of the world. If such personal authority is transposed into writing, this writing, standing alongside the original holy book, may begin to take precedence as the authoritative word. If such personal authority is passed on to a particular person or group of

80

persons who become the repository of authoritative interpretations, that person or group of persons will begin to take precedence as the authoritative controllers of the future of that group.

It is hard to imagine, for example, how the Jehovah's Witnesses could have survived without the authoritative interpretations of Charles T. Russell and J. F. Rutherford in a permanent written form for continued reference. Nor could one imagine the Christian Scientists surviving as a religious group without the authoritative writings of Mary Baker Eddy's book *Science and Health with Key to the Scriptures*. The Mormons have a strong central governing body to maintain the continuity of authority established around their founders, but even that governing body recognizes its dependence in turn on the writings of Joseph Smith and Brigham Young.

This authority creates a language of its own ... or more properly speaking, it usually reworks an old and familiar language. This becomes very confusing, for it essentially becomes a form of double-talk. People familiar with the original vocabulary are often caught off-guard by this new use of old familiar terms and they sense something strange about it while at the same time they are unable to identify just what it is that sounds so different.

Mary was a neighbor of ours years ago. She was a devout Christian and knowledgeable about her faith, a member of another denomination. She had a typical experience with this double-talk that may be helpful in illustrating our point here.

She came to me a few months ago telling of a visit by a pair of Jehovah's Witnesses. "I couldn't make heads or tails of what they were telling me about what they believe. They said they believed that Jesus was the Son of God, for example, but somehow through the whole thing I never quite felt that they and I were saying the same thing even with all those Scripture references."

Mary was pretty sharp in her observations. Perhaps someone with a little less theological intuition than she would have simply gotten upset over the persistence of the Jehovah's Witnesses, but Mary was honestly trying to listen and understand because she had heard a lot of things about the teachings of this group and this was the first time she had had a real chance to sit down and talk with them directly. It was not their persistence that bothered her, but their answers.

She was a pretty good student of the Bible herself and had a fairly strong understanding of Christian thought. That was why, although she found it hard to uncover directly, she sensed something very unsettling about what she was hearing. The Jehovah's

Witnesses have a doctrine of Christ that is essentially the same as one of the oldest heresies known to Christendom. It is their understanding that Christ is the closest manifestation we humans will ever have of God, although He is not Himself true God. Christ is entirely a creature, the highest of all creation and therefore closest to God, but not "of one substance with the Father" as the Nicene Creed speaks of Jesus. It was against this heresy (known as the "Arian heresy" after Arius, who first proposed it) that the Nicene Creed was formulated, in fact.

Once such an understanding of Jesus is established, of course, then all kinds of other understandings are rearranged, for also the meaning of words like Savior, sin, God, and many such ordinary and standard words in Christian vocabulary take on different definitions when faith in who Jesus is becomes redefined.

That is what made Mary so uneasy. She was hearing a very old heresy even though most of the vocabulary was familiar to her and even though the Bible was being quoted at every turn. This is characteristic of cults. Cultic teachings are masterful at subtly turning familiar things into error without ever letting a listener know what is happening. The combination of familiar language and familiar Scriptures traps many people into thinking these are just harmless fanatics rather than people who have laid hold on teachings long ago rejected by the Christian faith and who now wish to reintroduce them as legitimate understandings of Scripture. Most people are more disturbed by the stubborn way they insist on getting a hearing than they are by what they say, but that can be misleading. It is necessary to recognize the deeper problem that moved Mary to come to me in the situation described.

Such use of vocabulary, of course, requires considerable "double-talk," since it twists an original meaning from its earlier intention to the new intention held by those who use the word in a different way. Years ago a member of a parish I served joined the Mormon church. Since the "conversion" had been swift and complete before I even had wind of what was happening, I realized that my visit to their home was little more than a formality. Yet I felt it important to visit with them one last time.

Sam was not a casual member of the Lutheran Church before his conversion to the Church of Jesus Christ of Latter Day Saints. He was a very active and extremely knowledgeable member of the church, who had taken considerable pains through the years to acquaint himself with the formal body of Lutheran teachings as contained in the Book of Concord.

That was why I had to take seriously his statement, "I am not leaving the Christian faith. I still hold it as my commitment. It is just that I have found the warmth of the Mormon fellowship, their intense call to commitment, and their strong emphasis on family a more complete way to exercise my Christian commitment."

I tried to suggest that, being quite new to the Mormon fellowship, he may not entirely understand at that point all that was implied in their teachings. I mentioned the redefinition of terms that takes place ever so subtly and warned against being too quickly fooled by usage of familiar vocabulary and Holy Scripture, which in its turn is made subject to the interpretive postures of the Book of Mormon.

Had Sam been only a casual member of the church I could have said that he had, as the common expression puts it, "the wool pulled over his eyes." Here was a knowledgeable member of the church, however, insisting that nothing had changed essentially in terms of faith patterns. The only essential changes were a fellowship of firmly committed people surrounding his family with great warmth and encouraging the life of his own family to a new warmth of its own.

I know from an acquaintance with a mutual friend of Sam and myself that conversation and correspondence following the family's move showed an emphatic shift from the confession of faith considered orthodox in the circles of Christendom to new bases and new content. Our mutual friend shared a number of growing concerns he had as the correspondence became less and less interested in the primary thrusts of Christianity and obviously much more concerned with new and different areas of belief at considerable variance from that which I had known in Sam. I am not at all sure Sam himself ever realized how drastic this shift was, although he must have been aware of some considerable changes in his approach to faith and life. Whether he has ever realized to this day, though, that his commitment has shifted slowly and imperceptibly but very really to an entirely new type of commitment is probably subject to question.

How does this happen? It is basically the "double-talk" of which we have been speaking that enables it. Slow and subtle changes of definition of words and phrases under the influence of a group that is willing to retain old and familiar kinds of talk while meaning new and different things with it is a powerful force. It is an old trick in human history, by no means confined to religion! Its very force lies in its subtlety, and that is the reason one does well to test such "uneasiness" as we mentioned in Mary earlier anytime one is approached with a form of religious expression that somehow puts one on edge.

Of course, we must quickly recognize that something spoken of in unfamiliar language is not automatically wrong. Denominations develop particular ways of saying very standard things and therefore one denomination's way of saying the same thing may sound quite unfamiliar to a person from another denomination. We raise this caution lest unfamiliar language be equated too easily with cultic teachings.

Yet cults are quite expert at the kind of "double-talk" that is very convincing to a casual listener, and Christian people need to be deeply aware of this.

The reason this point is so easily missed is because quite a number of "newsworthy" cults appear so bizarre by the time they are newsworthy that the average Christian wonders how anybody could ever have bought the line of the cult to begin with.

The Jonestown event is a classic case in point. The question was on virtually everybody's lips as to how one man could convince that many people to commit suicide with him in a cause as strange as that which characterized the People's Temple movement. Why did people get involved in the movement to begin with . . . why did they stay with the movement . . . and why did they commit suicide simply because he told them they should?

"Religion by authority" is seen in its most undisguised form in that particular incident. Most of the elements we have been talking about were present in one way or another.

Jones's activity probably began as a movement not all that far removed from the life and thought of standard Christianity. Over the course of time, however, a combination of things evidently happened to transform the marginally Christian proclamation into quite a different form of religious expression. Rarely did this appear on the surface, of course. He fooled many people with the kind of "double-talk" that turned standard and even seemingly extraordinary human concern into a self-serving cadre of dedicated and devoted followers. Those who worked with him or heard him only on the surface levels of his activity were convinced of his authenticity, and his endorsements came from the highest levels of government. Even the church body that ordained him had no direct quarrels with him. On closer inspection they may well have had some questions about his teaching and activity, but on the surface nothing untoward indicated the deep-seated separation that had taken place between his movement and any resemblance to ordinary expressions of faith and life, whether in the church or out of it.

"What happened to Jones in his own private Christian pilgrimage will probably never be fully known.... Few disagree that by the time he reached Ukiah in 1965 he was only pretending to be a Christian, using the language and forms of faith and his apparent Christian social concern as a means to gaining power and a place in history.

"Over the years Jones became a master in his use of Christian trappings. On the door above the Temple in San Francisco, the sign still hangs advertising the People's Temple Christian Church, affiliated with the Disciples of Christ. . . . And the unsuspecting people who had heard the promises from Jones and his People's Temple, who had read complimentary stories in the San Francisco press, who had seen Jones's picture on television and in the newspapers with the famous and the powerful, knew only that they were entering an allegedly Christian church, affiliated with a respectable denomination, headed by an ordained Christian pastor." *(Deceived,* by Mel White. Spire Books, 1979, pp. 38, 39.)

Converts were not sought by putting forth strange and unusual notions, but by using language and concerns common to all. This language and these concerns were very subtly shifted into new meanings and areas of interest, however, by a man who demanded ultimate and total allegiance to himself. The story of how he maintained such a position of power and prestige over a rather long period of time is intriguing in itself. The totality of his authoritarian hold on the people who gained admittance to the inner core of his followers, however, is most vividly portrayed in the pictures of the hundreds of corpses lying around him in Jonestown. Typically cultic, Jones had manufactured a "religion by authority" that had gradually but most really sucked hundreds and thousands of people into total allegiance to his personal control.

The People's Temple became newsworthy primarily when it displayed a terrifying face to the world. One must not assume that all cults have as terrifying a face as Jonestown, for many of them have indeed a true decency about them that is praiseworthy. That does not make them more Christian or more true to whatever religious parentage they may have had, but one must recognize that some cults achieve a well enough established place in society to maintain themselves as authentic religious expressions all on their own.

That does not make them less a "religion by authority," though. For the cult lives and thrives off that basic central factor of a strong leader or a special authoritative writing that gives it legitimacy in its own eyes. That authority in most cases is far-reaching. It goes beyond statements of faith to entire modes of life.

Until not too long ago the most obvious form of that was to be found in the Hare Krishna cult, an offshoot of Hinduism. Its members were distinguished by their saffron robes and shaved heads save for the one strand of pigtail down their back. Their life together was and still is governed very strictly in local communal quarters even though in public they have now begun appearing on occasion in more standard clothing and hair styles. One cannot be a member of the Hare Krishnas without submitting the whole of one's life to the discipline fostered and maintained in their common life together, a life very highly regimented in virtually every way from diet to worship to waking and sleeping hours.

Probably even more celebrated among contemporary cults are the so-called Moonies, members of The Unification Church. A Christian background hangs behind the teachings of this group, although twisted and shaped to fit the needs of its founder and authoritarian leader, Sun Myung Moon. Again one could speak of definitions of familiar terms and phrases, showing how they have been reworked until they bear no real semblance anymore to the content with which they were originally filled.

Our concern at this point, however, is more the regimented style of life imposed on those who are followers of this man. "Religion by authority" recognizes that intense discipline of the followers is an important part of maintaining group loyalty. Moon demands total devotion from his people, making communes available for their day-by-day living, requiring of them in turn the relinquishment of any savings and personal property they may possess. Their time is tightly scheduled so as to insure that their every waking moment is filled with the remembrance of the man who requires their devotion and upon whom they have been made wholly dependent. It is Moon who selects marriage partners for them and must himself be involved in their marriage ceremony.

When one sees them tirelessly selling flowers or candles or some such thing on street corners, in parking lots, at centers for public transportation, and other such places, one wonders what could possibly possess people to give themselves so wholeheartedly and totally in devotion to a cause and a man as suspicious as this.

Why do people join *any* cult, for that matter? What possesses them to give such an outpouring of energy and such a total commitment to a cause that, to the average person, sounds and appears to be absurd?

Surely there must be as many answers to that question as there are people who join cults! Yet at least a couple of general observations that have fairly universal application can be made here.

One reason, surely, is the intense loneliness that so many people experience today. It is a common observation among youth—although older people are keenly aware of it also—that love, warmth, and strong commitment are sadly lacking in many (probably one should say *most!)* "mainline" denominational parishes. Much as one could wish otherwise, this observation has much truth in it.

It is precisely at this point where cults make their strongest inroads. Their initial approach is frequently made where loneliness is most keenly felt. Airports and other such travel terminals, the streets of impersonal cities, or other places where one is surrounded by people become the very settings where one is most vulnerable to feelings of great loneliness. So many people and not one friend! So much hurry and nobody to care!

It is there where the members of cults encounter prospective members, surrounding them with care and concern and acceptance. Only after they have been taken under wing and given a place to stay and people to care for them, a place that they come to feel offers more love than they have ever experienced before, are they completely exposed to the indoctrination and double-talk that would have been rejected almost out of hand at any earlier time. Only when they have been secured in such bonds of openly apparent concern are the harsher demands of discipline and lifestyle imposed on the unwary person.

Had you asked that same person earlier whether he/she would ever consider joining a cult, the answer would very likely have been an immediate and unqualified "no." Once caught up into such a net of security that comes from a community of people who have convinced you that you are very special and important to them and that here, above all places, you can find love and warmth such as you have never before experienced, the "yes" comes much more easily . . . almost without reflection and almost by instinct. The authority has become a "love figure," and his demands are the road to happiness! The double-talk makes sense in such circumstances even though it would never have made sense without the initial experiences of acceptance and community.

Another reason people are willing to submit to "religion by

authority" in the cultic forms lies in the great complexity of our age. Technological innovations coupled with a number of other forces have made choices available to us today such as have never before been experienced in the history of mankind. People who had few or no choices about things for which we have options today frequently longed for a wider number of alternatives. When we today are suddenly bombarded with what appear on occasion to be almost numberless alternatives in life-style, wide variations of ethical possibilities, and choices in almost any area of life one cares to speak of, decision-making becomes extremely difficult. How does one choose out of all the options open to every decision? An "easy" way to resolve this dilemma is to find someone who can seem to give you security, answers, a place where you can know you are cared for, and all the things you long for and have found so hard to find. In short, you may try to solve your problems by seeking some authoritarian person or position where you don't have to worry about things anymore. Better to let someone else do the worrying so long as that person establishes you in reasonable security, gives you a relatively sure future, and satisfies whatever needs you feel you have. "Religion by authority" works very well for people in such a situation, and our uncertain times have bred many children and adults with such a sense of insecurity that they gladly and willingly surrender themselves to the authority of anybody who can relieve them of the bewildering insecurities that have surrounded them.

Any base of security will do for many people, but if it has a religious foundation to it, all the better. Cults thrive in this kind of climate. "Religion by authority" seems perfectly suited for people who feel caught up in situations such as I have described. The problem, though, is that with the controlled atmosphere inside a cult it is hard to maintain ordinary powers of judgment. The double-talk takes its toll and leads one away from sound Christianity almost before one has realized it. The ultimate word becomes that of the leader or writing that requires the allegiance of the group, and all former commitments must give way.

This accounts, in its turn, for the highly conditioned responses one gets when trying to enter into dialog with members of cults. One discovers rather quickly that, if given the chance, they portray their groups in words that almost remind one of memorized recitation. They are rarely open to general questions and discussion, preferring to pose or rephrase your questions in such a way that it meets their needs, answering in turn with what seems to be a rather stock set of answers that they can make reference to. After all, if all answers come from an authoritative source, one cannot discuss in the same kind of open forum that we usually think of in the give and take of everyday conversation. One must keep answers straight in a world of quite different logic from that with which the average person works, and such answers need strong points of reference outside normal experiences of reality. In other words, they need an "authority" that rests beyond anyone's ordinary methods of proving or disproving the rightness or wrongness of what is being spoken about.

Therefore faith and life systems bred under "religion by authority" must work within certain frames of reference established by the cult. Any attempt at asking questions or carrying on conversation within the thought references ordinarily employed in the world of reality the average person experiences is simply not possible. The cult member lives, to all intents and purposes, in quite another world from that which the average person encounters. To provide for that, cults must carefully surround their members with environments suitable to maintaining credibility, to sustaining the pattern of thought imposed on the cult member, and to living in accordance with the system of belief imprinted on the member's mind and heart. Such a controlled environment will provide controlled responses to questioning, for free discourse is threatening to the welfare of any "religion by authority."

Much of this is sealed and secured by the intense sacrifices many cults require of their members. The more one has invested in the effort, the less likely that person is to leave the cult—or at least the harder it becomes for the person to renounce it. Sacrifice is both the "test" of loyalty and at the same time the "seal" of the commitment "religion by authority" is constantly seeking. A bond is thereby established between the participant and the authority whom he/she is serving so totally.

When cults mature (as some of them do even though the vast majority of them die rather quickly either at the death of the leader/authority or shortly thereafter), some of these characteristics begin to flatten out and become less evident. That happens because maturity brings with it a bit more respectability than was accorded to the cult previously and a growing confidence that members of the cult (now turning into a religious form of its own) can answer for themselves. As a maturing cult has to come to grips with a continuing life in the middle of the world rather than a transient life at the edge of the world, it must learn to speak to some of the realities the average person confronts. That forces some of its religious expression out of its shell and back again into an arena more strongly in touch with the world around it.

At times, then, a cult is forced by this turn of events to move back again into closer proximity to the parenting religion from which it originally separated. Frequently at times like this divisions begin to take place within the cult itself over such "temptations" to seek respectability and a hard core nucleus returns to cultic settings while others continue their journey in and around the borders of respectability.

That's one reason why many people become quite confused about what to think of cults. One can sense their distance and yet on occasion one feels their strivings to gain respectability among those who can, as it were, give them status in the society within which they exist.

Lest this chapter sound terribly judgmental, the reader needs to be keenly aware that major religious movements of today were in many instances considered cults in their origins. Christianity appeared to be a cult of Judaism. Islam appeared to be a cultic joining of Christianity and Judaism. Buddhism appeared to be a cult of Hinduism. One could continue to name such "departures" from an original parent that blossomed into full-blown religious systems of their own. That continues to happen today with some bodies that were cultic in origin but have found or are finding their way into the world as established systems of religious thought in their own right.

When one describes cults as we have been doing and then looks carefully into a mirror, do we not find resemblances to our own faith there? Is "religion by authority" foreign to any religious system?

Does not Christianity assume that Christ is the basic authority for all its teachings? Was He not considered "heretical" in His day by large numbers of people, including a majority of the religious leaders of Palestine? Were not holy writings accepted as authoritative interpretations of His life and teachings and work? Were not Old Testament terms taken up and used in forms that were filled with new content through faith in Christ? Cults seem utterly illogical to us, but does not our faith deal with matters that are far above and beyond reason? If the doctrines of our faith were "logical," why would it take the Spirit's work to convict us of their truth? Does not this faith move us to live a life-style in keeping with it, and are not our worship services at least in part designed to help us define and maintain a life-style consistent with Christian teaching and faith? Is not our vocabulary richly shaped by Biblical authority?

The point of this is not to call Christian faith into question, but rather to show that everything we can say about "religion by authority" in some way or another must be taken seriously. Members of cults are not to be considered wild-eyed or hare-brained! They are people like you and me who have found in an authoritative system of teaching and life a meaning that gave fulfillment to their lives, whether temporarily or permanently. It is not ours to judge them as people.

We can, however, and must judge the *systems* that hold people in their grasp. The same kind of questioning judgment must be turned back on ourselves as we ask what makes our "authority" more credible than that of others? How is our faith filled with divine life in ways that cultic faith is left empty?

Such questions find their ultimate response for Christian people in the Risen Christ. If a Man found His way through the treacherous path of death and returned to life by the grace of the Father who sent Him into death, that Man must surely be the connecting link to God, the ultimate authority. Anyone who holds the roadmap through death surely understands what life is all about! We speak of Jesus as the Lord of life precisely because He has clearly showed Himself to be the Lord of death.

The words we have that tell us about this Christ, including all that paved the way for Him as well as the interpretations of what His life and death meant for the life and death of the world, are included in the book to which we turn as our only source for authoritative teaching, the Holy Scriptures. That written Word about the Word made flesh is our instructor and guide for faith and life. For Christian people it is, indeed, the most trustworthy of all books because it is the Word from Him who founded the world with a word and will likewise end the world with a word.

Christian faith, then, is grounded in the authority of God, revealed in Christ, and given to us through the words of the prophets and apostles. It is trustworthy as our authority, and therefore the judge of all other authority, for in it we find the One who has overcome death and restored life. What authority can be more unfailing than that of One who has defied and overcome the powers of death?

It is the faith of Christian people that such authority lies behind their assertions. So we turn to "religion by faith" as our closing consideration in this book.

7

Religion by Faith

Kyrie eleison!	Lord have mercy!
Christe eleison!	Christ have mercy!
Kyrie eleison!	Lord have mercy!

This ancient cry of the church—one of the oldest remnants of liturgy still used by the church today—encapsulates so much of what "religion by faith" is about that we use it as the frame of reference for this entire chapter.

If we have said repeatedly that various forms of religious expression need to be warned about lest they become in themselves misleading, there should be some sort of way to speak of the Christian faith that incorporates the heart and core of Christian thinking throughout all ages and that can still serve as the measure for that faith today. One may lay hold on various forms of such confession of faith that have withstood the test of time, but none will serve us any better for the purposes of this final chapter than that time-tested and true cry of Christian faith:

> Kyrie eleison!
> Christe eleison!
> Kyrie eleison!

In this cry the church recognizes both its own frailty and also the frailty of the world within which its life must be sustained. All mankind stands helpless and vulnerable before forces that would crush its very humanity. In our dreams we wish and hope this is not so, but the reality of experience tells us it is a truth that will not be denied.

We try to ward off these threatening forces by gaining knowledge, for in knowledge is power. If we know the secrets of the universe, then we can gain power over them . . . or at the very least they will no longer appear as mysterious dragons suddenly swooping in on us from the unknown. But the secrets of the world elude our best efforts to know them. The mystery of the world heightens as we get to know it better and better!

The material world is a clear example. In spite of our best efforts at piercing the mysterious secrets of atoms and galaxies, the mystery of the universe expands instead of shrinking! Every "discovery" is as much a discovery of how much more there is to learn as it is a discovery of the foundation stones of material existence. The paradox is plainly this: The more we know the less we know. Beyond our knowledge lie deeper secrets and mysteries than we had ever imagined.

The mystery only deepens as we enter the world of morality. The harder we struggle toward a higher morality, the more we discover what a spider's web of ambiguity surrounds us. Increased knowledge of ourselves and our world does not lead us to become increasingly good people. We learn only to disguise our failures a little better—until our problems catch up with us in one giant flame of disaster. What appears to be good turns to blood in our hands. Our strongest efforts at doing right and good things are constantly tainted with a sinfulness that corrupts even the best of our deeds. Every time we are sure we have ascertained the difference between right and wrong and have set our foot on the right, we are thrown back into the ambiguities that bewilder us. Morality is established on and determined by a Power that understands life far better than we who seem so blind and unknowing even when we have plumbed our deepest wisdom.

Our very humanity is a most mysterious thing. What goes together to make a person what he/she is? We are told the possibilities for human development are almost as infinite as the sands. Yet our human path has taken so many detours from the potential that we sense lies within us that one must wonder what lies behind this never-ending struggle for realization. What is at our fingertips is at the same time light years away from us. What prevents us from "arriving" at even a fraction of the possibilities that are obviously available to the human creature?

If our humanity is such a mystery, then surely the divine mystery is overwhelming. Where or how can we discern the eternal mind of our Creator? How shall we answer the multitude of questions He addressed to His servant Job (Job 38—41) with the best of our modern knowledge? Will we ever be able to contain within our finite minds the infinite knowledge of Him who guides a universe... and yet calls us His children and knows us by name? Is it possible to hope for or even proper to pray for knowledge so great as that?

In short, can we ward off the forces that surround us and threaten to destroy us from within and without by increasing our knowledge? Surely that knowledge is for our Father alone, and not for His children.

For them the mysteries of the world known only to God bring forth a cry of faith rather than a prayer for knowledge. They utter a cry that may sound like despair to an unbeliever although it is really a cry of trust as we contemplate the awe-inspiring storehouse of wonder that makes up the universe we call home:

> Lord have mercy!
> Christ have mercy!
> Lord have mercy!

In that cry of humble dependence on the mercy of God the church confesses its confidence that the mercy of God has been revealed in the Christ. We cry for His mercy, not as though to an otherworldly God so transcendent that He is beyond our reach, but rather to the Lord who is known in the Christ.

The church is rooted in the world which God created. It is into such a world that He touched down in the person of Jesus of Nazareth. If we are to cry to the Lord for mercy, it must be enfleshed or it will only be a theoretical mercy. One does not confess faith as one espouses philosophy and as one may speak of theoretical hopes. Faith is more than humanistic compassion held high in moralistic teachings. Faith is based on the revelation of a God so gracious as to take up the stuff of this world into His own existence and expose Himself to the elements of this world in the form of a child in Bethlehem.

Such a God must be concerned with more than judgment, for the trouble and turmoil of our life are more than a distant thing to be observed by Him in disinterested fashion. They become the place where He takes up His abode. The world is the place where He is now to be encountered.

To call upon Christ for mercy, then, is to recognize in the cross the place where all history finds its ultimate focus. There the seeming finality of those forces suggested earlier as threatening to engulf and destroy us, as they are seen most openly exposed in death, work their most severe punishment on the second Adam. They give no quarter, and He takes up into Himself their worst blows in that strange mortal combat in which the Creator becomes the whipping boy, the accuser becomes the accused, the Holy One becomes the one penalized for sin. There all the roles are reversed, and sin is given its day while God submits to its charges and accusations.

The day ended with God's Son in the grave.

Three days later the forces that put Him there were smashed. The powers of God's life forced death and all its allies to their knees in submission. The grace of God's heart revealed itself to sinful and fallen mankind. One who holds the powers of life and death in His hand must surely be taken seriously. He has at His disposal the keys to all that one could desire to have available to oneself in terms of understanding and living life.

To be sure, He who can claim life out of death must also have a word that can be our judge as well as our salvation, that can speak death as well as life. In Him all things have their final outcome.

If He would place Himself into this path of suffering that leads to the death common to all mankind, though, surely He wants to be more than our judge, does He not? There must be something about Him that offers life in the midst of death if He has been willing to travel this road. In the face of our dying He must be offering life. To Him we cry in hope:

Kyrie eleison!
Christe eleison!
Kyrie eleison!

Can grace such as this be meant for *us,* though? Is it not too much to hope for that God could shower *our* existence with refreshing life like this? That God is gracious is one thing. That He is gracious to *us* is quite another!

It is incomprehensible, in fact! If what we can see and examine is too great for us to comprehend, a mystery within which we live, that which we cannot see and examine is still further from our comprehension and understanding! God's grace is of such an order as this.

Who is it that grasps my hand and provides me guidance through the difficult voyage of life if it is not the Spirit of God? Were I merely living by the ambiguities of a shiftless fate, I would surely have been destroyed long ago. Who shelters and protects me from the chance dangers and uncertainties of life if it is not the Spirit of a gracious God? The sea is wide and the night is dark as I travel through life. My own knowledge and understanding is a poor compass for the journey. Yet I travel on as though protected and guided in ways I do not understand. Were it an alien spirit that guided me, leading me to a futile end, surely the journey would have been finished in disaster long ago, for I am helpless when the waves toss and the darkness of the night surrounds me. Only One who seeks my good could have preserved me safely on my voyage thus far.

This Spirit of God brings something quite other than knowledge to me as a support for my pilgrimage. One can only call it faith, a trust that the darkness of the night and the perils of the way cannot destroy me so long as I entrust myself to this guiding hand that leads me through life.

This faith is more than a hope against hope, though. It is more than wishful dreaming, more than just a human vision. How can it be described? Perhaps as a certainty without seeing or a confidence without proof of sign or sight. It is knowledge of a sort, but not knowledge such as we usually talk about in our human setting. Faith sees what it believes with a confidence that bewilders those who are set on believing only what they can see with their eyes. Faith sees with the heart what the hand of God points to and promises to give us.

How can we know so surely when there is no way to verify our faith with irrefutable evidence? Is it possible that faith is a delusion, a mirage that raises hope in the desert dreariness of life? Although many have said it was nothing more than that, a person of faith refuses to explain faith so easily or so lightly as all that. Such a person filled with the confidence instilled within by the Holy Spirit asserts truth as it has been revealed in the Christ without having verifiable proof at hand, and he/she is willing to stake all of life on those assertions of faith!

In the end, though, it is not any special or particular knowledge given by the Spirit that such a person of faith relies on. It is not self-confidence or humanistic optimism or proud assertions of special insights that a person of faith relies on. Purely and simply it is the confidence that Someone who has seized hold of our existence will hear our constant cry:

> Lord have mercy!
> Christ have mercy!
> Lord have mercy!

The cry is a prayer. Faith knows that it cannot be sustained by human reason or strength. It must look beyond and outside its own resources for both its origin and its sustenance. It must cry to the One who alone knows from whence we have come and where we are going.

The prayer of such a person sees realistically all around the countryside of the world the devastations that have been worked through the human enterprise. It sees plainly that humanity left to itself, is bent on self-destruction in the name of self-fulfillment!

And it sees further, for distresses have so filled the world that all our days are filled with grief. From within and without the signs flood human existence that without the mercy of God we shall be swallowed up by alien forces.

Sickness and death cry for relief.

The lonely and forsaken cry for restoration of community and love.

The poverty-stricken and powerless people of the world cry for a hand to hold them up in the quicksand of social injustices.

The cancer of sin eats away at humanity from within and without.

Definite shapes and forms emerge from this huge scene of need and trouble. Mothers and fathers, sons and daughters, husbands and wives, friends and neighbors, governments and institutions bear burdens such as we have been describing, and our prayers specify the needs and those who have the needs. We cry out for the descent of God's grace into the midst of our human frustrations and needs, specifying and identifying those places and people upon whom we ask for the mercy of the Lord to rest.

There is something bigger than the sum of the parts, however. Sickness and death are larger than aunts and uncles who are known by name, larger even than the sum total of all those who are sick and dying around us. Sickness and death seem almost to have a personality that is set loose to wreak havoc on the human scene, something that must be dealt with in ways extending beyond the names of those who are sick and dying. They—and we with them, as future candidates of the same distresses—are victims of something that takes us one by one, isolating us in its ravages while it destroys us as a whole.

The same thing can be said for all those forces that threaten us and overshadow us with the dark clouds of their presence. They are so real that St. Paul can speak of them as principalities, powers, rulers of the darkness of this world, and in other similar ways. These are more than mere accidental infringements on our humanity that happen upon us. They are forces that assault us and bind us as demonic powers. Something has laid siege to our existence and threatens to devour us one by one and as a whole unless something or Someone equal to that overwhelming power comes to our rescue and saves us.

Although we can name the needs they raise and name the people in whom we sense their particular assault, thus praying very specifically, our prayers must be larger than all that. They must expand themselves far beyond the specific and pray as Jesus taught us to pray, "Lead us not into temptation, but deliver us from evil." This is the prayer of a desperate person who feels the nearing approach of the powers of darkness, threatening one's very existence. It is the prayer of a person who, knowing that Christ has indeed overcome those powers of darkness and that He alone can secure us before the deadly foe, cries out day and night:

> Kyrie eleison!
> Christe eleison!
> Kyrie eleison!

The prayer of faith takes on the form of praise and adoration as it breaks forth in mighty statements of "Credo," "I believe!" Faith confidently expresses what we believe to be the underlying reality of our lives in spite of what our eyes see and our bodies experience.

This great "I believe" hovers over the whole life of the Christian.

It is the confession that a heavenly Father has made the heavens and the earth and keeps them in their course. It is the "I believe" that the Father is the Lord of life.

It is the confession that God was made flesh in the person of Jesus Christ. It is the "I believe" that Jesus of Nazareth was the Savior of humanity.

It is the confession that God is the Source of faith and hope through the loving and gracious work of His Holy Spirit. It is the "I believe" that faith is entirely and totally the gift of God's Spirit.

Faith is to live without sight and yet to confess that it sees most certainly what God has set into motion and is bringing to pass. Faith is to live in the full awareness that although it knows nothing of great significance so far as knowledge is generally measured in this world, it knows this one thing only—that there is One who governs the course of the world and of our life in the person of God the Father, Son, and Holy Spirit. To entrust all things to His gracious providence is to cry daily:

> Lord have mercy!
> Christ have mercy!
> Lord have mercy!

Religion by faith, therefore, does not pretend to have any particularly preferred access to the hidden secrets of what God intends for the future other than the one great confidence that Christ will return to judge the quick and the dead in His own due time. It anticipates one thing only—that the grace and love of God are unfailing for those who love Him. This mercy of God that covers even the darkest of our sins has been promised from the beginning of the world and has now been made available in Jesus Christ, who shall one day receive us again unto Himself.

Beyond that kind of anticipation we move into presumptuousness, attempting to unravel the mysteries of God in ways He has never asked us to do nor given permission for us to do. The unfolding of His creative work remains hidden in the depth of His being, and it will be shown to us in due time. It is enough to be able to rest assured in His grace and to know that it will be there when He returns again just as it is available to us now in our daily living.

We live by faith, not by knowledge, and faith leads us to say:

> Kyrie eleison!
> Christe eleison!
> Kyrie eleison!

Faith is called into being through the seeming weakness of the Word of the Lord. When we look for the surge of God's power rushing upon us, we find it in the quiet places of the written Word and of water, bread, and wine. The wisdom of God appears among us as foolishness to men. Those who watch the heavens, scanning them to see the day of His coming, are surprised at finding that while their eyes were turned toward the heavens God's glory was revealed in a stable where His Word was made flesh, and His grace was made available on a cross, where His dying was made our life.

Where humans look for strength, God appears in weakness. When we want to proclaim His power, He comes in the stumbling-block form of servanthood. Into the simple everydayness of our mortal elements God pours out His grace and mercy for us to receive. As though He had no power, God enters His world and brings a fermenting change into everything through His powerless people who are committed to servanthood. Such weakness is not fitting for the God of the universe, some say. Kings must exercise power and authority!

Faith sees the strength in weakness and lives by the cross. It does not worry about power, but knows only how to say in deep humility:

Lord have mercy!
Christ have mercy!
Lord have mercy!

There is no sign for faith other than the sign of the resurrection. Even that cannot be proved. It can only be confessed. The conviction, though, that this one great "sign of Jonah," as our Lord described it, stands in the midst of human dying is enough. We need no other.

When and where God grants other signs, we receive them gratefully. We do not require them, though, nor do we seek them. We receive them when given, but we do not live by them. For we live by faith. Any sign God chooses to give us will be understood and interpreted only by the faith that came to us as a gift in the first place. So faith sustains our life, not signs. And faith cries always:

Kyrie eleison!
Christe eleison!
Kyrie eleison!

People of faith know they are held responsible for the faith given them. They are stewards of the grace of God.

They are never able to say, though, that the faith over which they must exercise responsible stewardship has come into being by virtue of their own strength or will. Faith is a gift, a greater gift than we could ever expect or hope for!

Everything we do, then, is given its original impetus by the Spirit of the Lord who has worked in ways mysterious to us. He has called our life and heart and will into His service. This is a great privilege! It was not our doing, and we can claim no honor in and of ourselves for the gift we hold.

Privileges are always two-edged, however. Calling for praise and thanksgiving on the one hand, our privilege is a call to responsible use on the other hand.

When we see the mountain of opportunity and possibility that confronts our responsibility, we are overwhelmed. There is but one cry that can sustain us in the face of this awesome task placed before us:

Lord have mercy!
Christ have mercy!
Lord have mercy!

Our faith is grounded in God's heart, not His head. It is His

100

heart that is revealed in the written Word of the Holy Scriptures. We have no other place to turn for guidance or understanding in regard to faith and life. What we read there is beyond our reason and understanding, it is admitted, for our heads cannot fathom the heart of God. It is virtually impossible to comprehend the length and breadth and width of the love that is revealed to us in this story of His mercy. The one truth of vital importance that emerges is that God in Christ has revealed an abiding love for His creation that cannot be shaken. In the middle of much that bewilders us, that one truth shines like a diamond, and all the rest of the message clusters around this one central kernel.

Faith recognizes, then, the necessity of preserving that one central truth by taking the whole of this revelation seriously. While guarding against making the Bible simply a divine rulebook or a book of godly logarithms which will help us solve human problems or a book of roadmaps through life, the person of faith sees in the whole of the Bible the story of God's continuing love. At times the story confounds us, and at times it fills us with awe. But always the book is devoted to the one theme that God's grace is available in the midst of human sin to those who desire new life, and this grace is our only hope. The Bible is dedicated to that truth.

Our faith, then, born of the Bible, is not a deciphering of secret messages from its many pages, but a hearing with open heart the good news of grace that shines through the whole of its story from Creation through the promise of the second coming of Christ. Not just a religion by the Bible, but a religion of the Bible, the Christian faith hears echoed from beginning to end the response of God's grace to the age-old cry of humanity:

> Kyrie eleison!
> Christe eleison!
> Kyrie eleison!

There is only one Master for faith born of the Lord—the God of Abraham, Isaac, and Jacob, the Father of our Lord Jesus Christ. Any authority that replaces Him is an idol, the work of human hands and hearts that will one day be overthrown. None can have His place.

We know that we are being misled, then, when we are asked to seek mercy at any hand other than the hand of this God whom we have come to know in the Christ. No one else can give us life. He who first breathed life into our dust and who gave His Son in order that life might again be restored to our dying bodies is alone entitled to our praise and adoration.

Yet, because we are so given to our own idolatries and so tempted to establish our own gods, we must always keep the cry on our lips:

Lord have mercy!
Christ have mercy!
Lord have mercy!

Our faith, however, is not "otherworldly." It is fastened down and sealed in the stuff of this earth. Just as Christ was rooted in human flesh and worked out God's will as a man even though His origins were from eternity, so also God gives material means to express and strengthen faith that is born of the Spirit's working.

He gives water—the plain stuff in which we wash and of which we drink and by which our very human life is sustained—and transforms it into the stuff of spiritual rebirth. What has been vital to physical life is made vital to spiritual life also! We are touched with heavenly grace in the midst of our human frailty when we are washed in water poured under the word and promise of God "in the name of the Father, and of the Son, and of the Holy Spirit." God's promise is sealed in the washing of plain, simple water poured upon us at His command.

How does water do such things?

As Martin Luther so wisely pointed out, "It is not the water indeed that does them, but the word of God which is in and with the water, and faith, which trusts such word of God in the water."

What kind of faith turns to such water and uses it? It is the faith that God has seen and knows our human dilemma, and that He has dealt with it according to the richness of His grace. It is a faith that knows our only hope from the human point of view lies in the cry:

Kyrie eleison!
Christe eleison!
Kyrie eleison!

If such a cry gives rise to the use of water with God's word as a material seal of His promised mercy, it should come as no surprise to find our lives pointed back again and again through the whole of our life to that One in whom this mercy of God was given through still other material means—the forms of bread and wine. All our hope for God's mercy centers in this One who has taken our suffering and death into Himself and has overcome death in resurrection. His body and blood is the focus of God's mercy and the vital center of His redemptive work.

"This is My body. . . . This is My blood." These words, said by Jesus over the bread and wine of the last Passover He celebrated with His disciples, become the pivotal point around which our remembering Jesus takes on its most vivid form. He promises to be present in our eating and drinking together in His name. We are confident, according to His word, that He who promised to be present with us when the bread and wine are presented as acts of faith is truly received by His people in the eating and drinking for the forgiveness of sins, life and salvation.

We turn to the bread and wine in our weakness and need because a promise rests over them from the lips of our Lord Himself. We know that He is present with mercy . . . and we know that we dare approach this table of the Lord with only one cry in our heart and on our lips:

> Lord have mercy!
> Christ have mercy!
> Lord have mercy!

One cry alone suffices to sound the faith of the church wherever that faith is practiced, however that faith is expressed, whoever is caught up into its sweep. That lone cry echoing the depths of our faith is:

> Kyrie eleison!
> Christe eleison!
> Kyrie eleison!

The critical questions that must be asked those who call themselves by the name of Christ revolve around this cry. Do we know that without the mercy of God given in the Christ we are a doomed people? Do we realize that our utter helplessness has been seen and caught up into the merciful hands of God? Are we aware that one who will not speak the "Kyrie, eleison" has shut him/herself off from the God of mercy?

The church's liturgy echoes and reechoes this cry precisely because it is the deepest cry of the Christian heart, the deepest expression of the Christian faith. That is why the refrain has been used to frame the thoughts of this final chapter.

For it is all too easy to forget this cry in our desire to know the very thoughts of God. We would far more gladly look for magnificent displays of God's power rather than simply trust Him even when and especially when He appears in weakness and leaves us to the silent moments when there is no sign but the Word and water, bread, and wine. We all too readily seek certainty born of signs that assure us rather than living by a faith that knows only enough to cry daily, "Lord, have mercy!" He reveals Himself in and through words, but all those words in their turn point to the Word made flesh, in whom the mercy of God has been made available to us mortals. We are a people enabled by the mercy of God to do His works on earth because of this renewal in Christ.

This is what it means to live by faith . . . to rely on the mercy of God. Any time the cry for mercy is removed from the center of faith our Christian profession is endangered and God's work among us is jeopardized.

On the very evening when these final words of this book were written I was walking with an elderly aunt confined to a nursing home when I witnessed an event that was most striking to me precisely because of the thoughts we have just been sharing.

Another resident of the home was resisting attempts on the part of an aide to keep her from going in a certain direction. She had just successfully freed herself from the aide when another resident of the home coming down the hall attempted to prevent her once again from going where she wanted to go.

Arguing with the other resident, she said in anger, "Why does everybody pick on me?" Then, successfully freeing herself a second time from such attempts at restraint, she went her way down the hall quite obviously perturbed. Suddenly I heard her say loudly, "Lord, have mercy!"

Whether I read all sorts of things into her remark because I was thinking of this final chapter or whether she was indeed saying something of what we have been suggesting in these pages is hard to say. But, having observed what brought that remark on, spoken to nobody in particular but perhaps to anyone who might indeed deliver her from what she perceived as persecution, I could not help but think she spoke for hosts of people who feel constantly threatened by life and its many vicissitudes.

For she was saying, if I understood her at all, "Lord, have mercy! So many people and forces seem determined to stop me from the course I wish to take. I am surrounded by people who want to impose their will on me. Take my cause and hold it before Your eyes, O Lord. I shall be undone by these who surround me if it be not true that You can deliver me."

Although I will freely grant that this particular woman would never have said all those things just like that, her cry came down the hall to me as the cries of God's children come to Him out of the experiences of daily life on earth.

We are healthy and whole only when this ancient cry of the church, echoed by this woman in her pathetic dismissal of all who stood between her and her wish to go a certain way down a hall, is repeated over and over again as the sole hope in our living and in our dying:

Kyrie eleison!	Lord have mercy!
Christe eleison!	Christ have mercy!
Kyrie eleison!	Lord have mercy!

This is the cry of faith!

The cry "Lord have mercy" is a cry of confidence in the midst of the harsh realities of life to a God who Himself lives and offers life! The cry for mercy is not an empty cry of despair to an empty void, but it is the expression of hope that rises from the heart and life of people who have seen the shadows of the cross overcome in the glory of Easter morning! "Lord have mercy" is the upbeat cry of a person who is convinced that death has met its Master. It is the cry of a person beset on every side by the dying-ness of this world, but who nevertheless defies death in the name of the Lord of the living and cries for life in the middle of death.

Thus we must always remember that the cry for mercy is the prelude to the second cry that follows ... a cry that can be uttered in its fullest meaning only by a person who has encountered angels at Christmas. For it is *their* song that follows hard on the heels of *our* cry for mercy:

Gloria in excelsis Deo!
Glory to God in the highest!

When a person has learned to say "Kyrie eleison" in the middle of the living that is dying and has been offered a life bigger than death itself, one cannot settle for downbeat faith or life. Where God's mercy has been revealed and offered, the joyful song of praise scatters all the darkness of fallen reality, saying:

Gloria in excelsis Deo!

Where lives have been touched by Jesus Christ so that the harsh realities of the suffering that make up so much of life have been taken up into the cross, a transformation takes place. The suffering and dying to which we are exposed become instead the refining and sifting that expose the grandeur of God's grace in the whole of creation even in the midst of the shambles we have made of it with our sin. There the cry must go up loudly:

Glory to God in the highest!

It is the angels' song given to us poor mortals! It is the heavenly song made available to us already here on earth to be sung by faith! It is the song of joy that only forgiven and renewed lips can sing on this earth, for it is the song that joins the grace of our heavenly Father to our human lives that are daily crying for mercy:

Gloria in excelsis Deo!

Where such a song is found in one's heart and on one's lips, there must first of all be the awareness of our humanity that cries out:

Kyrie eleison!
Lord have mercy!

In such a hungering and thirsting after righteousness, though, we have been assured by Jesus that we shall be filled and satisfied with the divine mercies poured out with richness from above. And thus we dare to sing in the middle of our mortality and finiteness the song of eternity where our perishing shall be made imperishable and our dishonor shall be changed into glory and our weakness shall become empowered by God Himself. If the cry of our humanity perhaps sounds somewhat downbeat because of the harshness of the reality that shadows all our dying, then let us cry out with the angels the upbeat song that shall ring throughout the eternal mansions forever:

Gloria in excelsis Deo!
Glory to God in the highest!
This is the song to which faith leads!

Discussion Questions

Religion by Anticipation and Fulfillment

1. One of your close friends comes to you and tells you that on the basis of a new Bible study program she has been introduced to (emphasizing such books as Daniel, Ezekiel, and Revelation), she has concluded that the end of time will come at a point in the near future, and she has gone so far as to identify that point specifically. On the basis of this new insight she intends to quit school and do intensive evangelism work. How will you respond to her?

2. What is the Biblical definition of prophecy? How will this definition of prophecy help you evaluate claims of prophecy today?

3. In what sense is Jesus Christ the center of prophecy? Of both predictive Biblical prophecy and legitimate prophecy today?

4. In some respects the call to anticipate the imminent end of this age is necessary. The Christian always needs to be ready for Christ's second coming. What are some of the ways we are to prepare ourselves?

5. To what do the prophecies concerning Israel in the New Testament refer? You may wish to ask your pastor for help here.

6. How does the overall purpose for which the Bible was given help us to understand the prophetic sections and keep us from fanciful, speculative interpretations?

7. What are the two primary intentions of Biblical prophecy? How are these twin intentions as equally relevant for us today as they were for the people to whom they were first addressed?

8. How would you interpret Peter's statement that the prophets themselves searched intently trying to determine the time and

circumstances within which their prophetic word would be fulfilled (1 Peter 1:10)?

9. Read Matt. 24:36. What does this passage say to those who would calculate the divine timetable for the end of the age?

10. Review: Formulate a summary statement defining Biblical prophecy; specifically, pay attention to its intent and its central message, as well as to those things which prophecy is not intended to teach.

Religion by Unconcealed Power

1. Millennial notions thrive at times of social, economic, and political unrest and insecurity. Cite some of the factors present today which contribute to current ideas of "religion by unconcealed power."

2. Do you believe it is valid to claim that some Biblical promises specifically made to Israel have never come true? If they have come true, what was/is the nature of that fulfillment? Refer to the previous chapter to help you answer.

3. How would you define "religion by unconcealed power"? What are some of the ways it manifests itself in the popular religious sphere today?

4. What would you identify as the fundamental error of those who formulate ingenious schemes by which to calculate the end time, and who literalistically wring from Scripture every conceivable clue in order to draw a full blueprint of what will happen at the end of history?

5. Based on what you know about millennial groups and their rather selective interpretive procedures, what do you think they would identify as the most important article of the Christian faith? Do you agree or disagree?

6. Do you believe the charge of "fatalism" actually applies to millennial groups? Explain your answer.

7. What effect will strict millennial notions have on one's application of the Gospel to social concerns that arise? Will one be more or less ready to respond to needs for social ministry? Perhaps your discussion of fatalism will help you here.

8. What is the basic purpose for which God gave us the Bible? How does this purpose square with the efforts of certain individuals to discover the blueprint for the future?

9. On the basis of what you have discussed concerning the purpose of the Bible and the chief article of the Christian faith, what is the root problem of those who espouse "religion by unconcealed power?"

Religion by Signs

1. In the first conversation related in the chapter, the young man stated that he felt uncomfortable about "putting his faith on the line like that." What do you think he meant? How would you feel if you went to such a healing meeting and nothing happened? Would your faith be affected? If so, how? If not, why not?

2. How do those who advocate a "religion by signs" view the role of prayer? How do *you* view the role of prayer as it pertains to deliverance from physical or psychological distress?

3. What was the principal function of signs and wonders as they were performed by Jesus or by the apostles in the early church? What is their function today?

4. What is the basic problem with a "religion by signs"? Is it centered in the action of God or man? Explain your answer.

5. What is the acid test of whether a sign is performing its proper, God-appointed function, or some other, man-made one? Look up 1 Cor. 12—14 to help you with your answer.

6. A close friend of yours tells you that she has prayed for and received the gift of speaking in tongues. She is exuberant about having received this gift. She urges you to pray for it, explaining that tongues are God's way of identifying and rewarding better or "more spiritual" Christians. Do you think she is correct? How will you respond to her?

Religion by Decision

1. Martin Luther kept a small sign on his desk saying: "I am baptized." The purpose of this little sign was to remind him in

moments of doubt that he was indeed God's redeemed child. How does Baptism serve that function? Elaborate on your answer.

2. Is Baptism primarily God's act or man's? Read Rom. 6:1-11 to help you answer. What implication does your answer have for the question of infant Baptism?

3. React to this statement: God's grace is a reward for man's spiritual preparation. See Eph. 2:8-9.

4. What are some of the dangers involved in stressing one's personal "decision for Christ"?

5. Even though we are all sinful, we nevertheless retain the freedom to choose for or against Christ. Is this statement true or false? Explain your answer. Look up Eph. 2:1 and 1 Cor. 12:3 and reflect on the implications of those passages.

6. How is the emphasis on "experiencing Christ" very similar to what we discussed in the previous chapter on "religion by signs"?

7. What is the source of our Christian comfort—God's decisive, objective act in Jesus Christ, or our experience of it? Explain.

8. Name the means by which God imparts His saving grace to us. The fact that God is the subject of the sentence has important implications for the role of man in the way of salvation. Discuss these implications.

9. Discuss what it means to be born again. Look up John 3:1-17; Rom. 3:21-28; and 2 Cor. 5:17-21.

10. Look up Luther's explanation to the Third Article of the Apostles' Creed and read it together as an excellent summary of the truths learned in this lesson.

Religion by the Bible

1. You overhear a conversation between two parties. One of them says that to try to demonstrate anything from the Bible is useless, because you can use the Bible to prove anything. How would you have responded if that remark had been directed to you?

2. If a person of another religious faith asked you to describe the Christian Bible, what would you tell him?

3. What is the danger involved in using the Bible as either a road map to the future or as a handy answer book to all of our pressing questions?

4. What is the overriding purpose for which God revealed the Holy Scriptures? Look up John 5:39; 20:31; and 2 Tim. 3:16-17 to help you answer. What are the interpretive implications of this purpose?

5. What is the difference between a "religion by the Bible" and a "religion of the Bible"?

6. Explain the importance of viewing each Scripture passage in its proper historical setting.

7. What do we mean by the expression "Scripture interprets Scripture"?

8. What is the importance of the fact that the Bible is the possession of the entire church? What role does the tradition of the church play in this connection?

9. How is the proper distinction between Law and Gospel the interpretive key for the correct understanding of Scripture?

10. What basic rule of thumb must we remember when interpreting the Old Testament, especially the prophetic passages?

Religion by Authority

1. A member of your congregation has joined a prominent contemporary cult, and you are assigned to call on him. He tells you that the reason he left the congregation was the absence of caring and support among the members. He claims, moreover, that he has found this warmth among his new group. If this were a real individual from your congregation, would he have been correct in his estimation? How would you respond to him?

2. Discuss the peculiar attraction that cult leaders seemingly hold over their adherents. To what do you attribute the longing for authority on the part of the members?

3. Give some examples of how cults use familiar terminology with

entirely new meanings. What must the Christian church do to combat this deception as it seeks to make inroads in our congregations?

4. What do you think is the most effective means by which to reach those ensnared in the clutches of one of the cults?

5. What is the crucial test which must be put to any group that claims the name "Christian"?

6. What is the one true authority we have and must cling to in all spiritual concerns?

Religion by Faith

1. What is the one, all-important "sign" or demonstration of how God really feels about us?

2. Reflect on how this "sign" is crucial in the midst of the low points of life—for example, times of depression, loneliness, or guilt.

3. Who is the Source and Sustainer of our faith? The proper answer to this question is very important when we experience doubt or insecurity about the validity or strength of our faith. Discuss in your group how this is so.

4. Explain and reflect upon the meaning and implications of this statement: Where humans look for strength, God appears in weakness.